CANCER, GOD, AND Me

CHRISTY ADAMS

COPYRIGHT © 2021	ii
DISCLAIMERS	iii
DEDICATION	iv
ACKNOWLEDGMENTS	v
PROLOGUE	7
ONE	9
TWO	25
THREE	33
FOUR	45
FIVE	53
SIX	65
SEVEN	71
EIGHT	79
NINE	87
TEN	95
ELEVEN	103
TWELVE	111
THIRTEEN	135
FOURTEEN	147
FIFTEEN	155
SIXTEEN	165
SEVENTEEN	181
EIGHTEEN	193
NINETEEN	201
TWENTY	207
EPILOGUE	211
CLOSE TO MY HEART BREAST CANCER FOUNDATION	215
ABOUT THE AUTHOR	218
REFERENCES	219

COPYRIGHT © 2021

CANCER, GOD, AND ME BY CHRISTY ADAMS

All rights reserved. No part of this book may be reproduced, distributed, or transmitted in any form or by any means or stored in any database or retrieval system without prior permission from the author.

The scanning, uploading, and distribution of this book via the internet or via any other means without permission of the publisher is illegal and punishable by law. Please purchase only authorized electronic or hard/soft cover editions and do not participate in or encourage electronic piracy of copyrighted material.

Editing, Interior Formatting, and Cover Design by
Silla Webb/Masque of the Red Pen

DISCLAIMERS

This book is not meant to be used to diagnose or treat any disease, nor should it be. Do your own research regarding any issues you may have. For diagnosis or treatment of any medical problem or illness, consult your own physician.

All dates in this book are approximate.

All Scripture used in this book is King James Version.

Names of doctors and medical staff have been changed.

DEDICATION

This book is dedicated, first and foremost, to Jesus, who rescued me out of the grips of the ugly monster of cancer. Without Him, this testimonial would not be possible. He is my all and all, my everything.

To all my "pink" sisters who have bravely fought breast cancer. Whether they won the fight or not, they fought and that is what matters!

To my son, Josh, there are not enough words in my vocabulary nor enough time in a day to tell you how much you mean to me. You stayed by my side all during my journey. You waited on me hand and foot. You slept in my room so you could watch over me, and you helped me to fight when I had no strength left. You are the true hero in this story. I love you more than you know.

To my friends who rallied around me in the darkest time of my life, thank you. I love you all. You will never fully realize what your support has meant to me. I pray that God returns the blessing to you many times over.

To my sister, Lisa, I love you. Thank you for calling me every day to make sure I was alright and encouraging me on the hardest days.

ACKNOWLEDGMENTS

To my oncologist, his nurse practitioner, all the chemo nurses, my radiation doctor, and all her nurses and to the receptionists who checked me in every day, I want to say a deep, heartfelt thank you. You were the sunshine that I needed on days that I felt I couldn't carry on.

To my surgeon who found the cancer in the first place because he saw something odd, thank you does not seem sufficient enough, but thank you.

Without all of you working together to take care of me, I would not be here today.

You all mean more to me than I could ever express.

To the receptionist who went above and beyond her job duties to get me to come in and get checked. I think of you often and how much you played a part in saving my life. Thank you.

And finally, to my church family, who prayed for me relentlessly and stood in the gap for me every day, thank you. I love you all more than you know.

"For I know the thoughts that I think toward you, saith the LORD, thoughts of peace, and not of evil, to give you an expected end."
-Jeremiah 29:11

Prologue

In every tragedy there are five stages through which an individual must move in order to get from one side of grief to the other. Each with its own set of difficulties; nevertheless, they all must be experienced if one is going to overcome the adversity she is facing.

The most common stages in any given situation of grieving are denial, anger, bargaining, depression, and acceptance. No two people experience the stages at the same time, in the same order, or move through them at the same speed. Why? Because no two people deal with grief the same way.

I have known twins who lost their mother and dealt with that loss differently. One sister moved through the grief at a rapid pace, while the other seemed to get caught and not be able to move forward for a time.

When I was diagnosed with breast cancer, I felt like I went through all the stages of grief at the same time. Of course, I am one who naturally plows through every obstacle in life very quickly because it's my personality to do so. After a couple of months, my emotions caught up with my mind, and only then did I begin to allow myself to truly experience each stage fully and completely. It took me an entire year to do that, and there are still times when I find myself struggling in a stage of grief.

If you are grieving right now, allow yourself to move at your own pace. Do not let anyone tell you how you are *supposed* to feel during this time or how to deal with whatever you are going through. That is yours alone to deal with in the way that comes most naturally to you. Do not try to speed up the process. Allow yourself the grace necessary to go at the pace you are going. You will get there, eventually.

Blessings to you,

Christy

One

The Lump That Wouldn't Leave

"And not only so, but we glory in tribulations also: knowing that tribulation worketh patience."
-Romans 5:3

Although this first part of the book is all about faith, I must start with what happened in the very beginning that got me to the point where faith became my top priority.

February 13, 2020 was the day I was diagnosed with stage 3, grade 3, triple negative infiltrating ductal carcinoma. Yeah, I know, that is a mouthful. It was a lot for me to take in when I first heard the words that day. Let me go back to the very beginning and explain what brought me to the place where the surgeon said those words.

CANCER, GOD, AND ME

August 2018 was a wonderful time for me. Actually, that entire year had been pretty fantastic. In January, my son and I had moved to the mountains of East Tennessee, a place I had loved visiting since he was three-years-old. I was working at my happy place, Dollywood, as a salesperson in an upscale home décor store where I met amazing people every day as I sold them Joanna Gaines look-a-like farmhouse furniture. I got to meet Dolly Parton in person, which was a dream come true because I had loved her from the womb; I mean, who doesn't love Dolly?

No, seriously, my first memories of Dolly were when I was about five-years-old, and my grandparents watched The Porter Wagoner Show. That was when I fell in love with Dolly Parton, the voice, the hair, and the sweet soul. I actually cried until my grandpa bought me their album and let me play it on his giant console record player; that was the early seventies, after all.

Anyway, while working at her park I got to know more about her than I ever thought I would, and I made some of the best friends I have ever known in my life. I was also enrolled in college, working toward my degree in psychology. It seemed my dreams were finally coming true.

Yes, life seemed perfect that beautiful summer day.

But I will never forget the moment it all changed. I was

CHRISTY ADAMS

sitting on my bed, doing my homework when I reached up to scratch an itch on my chest, just below my collarbone. I wasn't paying much attention to it as I read my textbook, but as soon as my fingers hit on a small lump at the top of my right breast, my world stopped. I instinctively began moving my hand around and felt a very tiny, hard spot that caused major panic in me. I had heard all my life about lumps and bumps, self-breast exams, early detection, and the like, and I had been having regular mammograms for ten years. I had taken care of my health fairly well over the years since I had turned forty.

Of course, in that moment of shock and panic, I reached for the phone to call my gynecologist's office to get in to see his nurse practitioner to have it checked. The irony of it is that I had literally just gotten home a few minutes earlier from an appointment with her for my annual pap smear. However, she did not do a breast exam that day, only the pap.

After a couple of rings, I looked at the clock on my laptop and saw that it was 4:59 pm. I figured they had stopped answering the phone for the day, and I would have to spend the rest of the night waiting anxiously for them to open the next morning.

Just when I was getting ready to hang up, a sweet voice answered, "Women's Healthcare Center, Dr. B's office."

CANCER, GOD, AND ME

Let me begin by saying that Dr. B is the sweetest doctor I have ever met. He is kind and has a gentle way about him when he speaks. He is a Christian who prays *with* and *for* his patients, which is really awesome if you ask me.

After explaining what I had just "discovered," I was told to be there at 9:00 a.m. the next morning so that his nurse practitioner could have a look at it. I called my boss and told her I would be late to work and why, and I went back to my textbook and finished my homework. Somehow, just knowing I had an appointment the next morning helped to ease my mind of anything actually being wrong. Or did it? Maybe it just took my mind off it for a while.

When I laid down that night, I could *not* get to sleep. I was thinking about the little lump that was only the size of a jellybean, and I somehow knew I had cancer growing inside me. I cannot explain to anyone when they ask me how I knew, but I just did. I have heard that it is fairly common among cancer patients to know instinctively, although none of us can explain why or how.

The next morning, I arrived early for my appointment, as if that would get me in sooner and stop the spread of whatever was happening in my body. As I sat there, I could feel my heart beating faster and my palms sweating. Every time the door opened and I heard a name called that wasn't mine, it felt as if the anxiety that was already flooding my being rose a level. With every passing minute the fear of the unknown was starting to get to me. I knew that if the nurse did not call my name soon, I was going to either leave and try to ignore it all, or I was going to ask the receptionist to get me back there. I was officially in flight or fight mode by that point.

It felt as if they were not as concerned as I was; maybe because I am sure they deal with that type of problem on a daily basis. But that was my first experience with a lump, and I was an absolute mess.

As soon as the nurse finally called my name, I stood quickly and followed her to the exam room. After waiting for a few minutes that felt like an eternity, the nurse practitioner came in and did the breast exam. She felt the lump and said it was probably only a fluid-filled cyst. She explained they are small, grape-sized sacs filled with fluid and are usually noncancerous and nothing to be concerned with unless it got bigger and became uncomfortable. She told me to come back to the office if it "grew," and they would go from there. She left me with a smile and a good luck, so I got dressed and almost skipped out of the office with the assurance that nothing was wrong. I mean, I had just gotten great news from the nurse practitioner, right? Except for the little gnawing in the pit of my stomach trying to let me know something *was* wrong, and I really *did* have cancer and not just a fluid-filled cyst. But hey, I'm not a doctor, and so I took what she said at face value and went back to my life of being happy at my happy place.

Fast forward two months to October 2018. The lump had grown to the size of a golf ball. It was sore, and I knew it was time to have it checked again. So I called the doctor's office and was given an appointment to come in the next day. One of the great things I can say about Dr. B and his staff is they don't make you wait. If you have an issue, they will fit you in almost immediately.

The nurse practitioner did another exam and measured the lump with a small cloth tape measure that looked like she had plucked it out of a sewing kit. She told me it *had* grown in size and I would need to get it aspirated, which is a fancy word for drained. She explained that the fluid would be sent to pathology to make sure it was not cancerous. I nodded in agreement and forced a smile, something I was very good at doing by that point in my life. But inside, I was petrified.

After waiting a couple of days for the call from the doctor's office, I finally had a date for my first aspiration. Yes, you read that correctly. The first of many aspirations that would take place over the next thirteen months.

CHRISTY ADAMS

The morning I arrived at the breast center, which is in the same building as my gynecologist's office, I was more nervous than I had been in a very long time. Let me take this moment to give you a fun fact. My love of Dolly Parton is not only due to her music and who she is as a humble human being, but also the fact that she is a humanitarian who gives back to the community in which she grew up. The medical center where my gynecologist office and the breast center are located is called The Dolly Parton Center for Women's Services. Dolly gave the money for this facility to be built so that women in this area could get proper healthcare. She is an extraordinary person to want to help those less fortunate. My heart will always love her for what she does and who she is.

I was taken to a room that looked like a regular exam room except it was larger and had a lot of needles and other medical apparatus the doctor would be working with during the procedure. There was soft 80's music playing in the background, in an effort to relax the patient, I'm sure. It certainly seemed to work for me. As I laid there listening to Cyndi Lauper belt out "Girls Just Want to Have Fun," I transported back to high school when my friends and I would ride around all weekend and sing and laughed. I couldn't help the smile that made its way across my face as I remembered the simple times in my life. The times when all I had to worry about was where we were going to eat instead of a lump in my breast.

I felt myself relaxing somewhat, and I began to look around the room. It was pretty. I realize that sounds odd to say about a room where I was about to have a procedure done, but it was nice. The walls were painted a soft hue of light blue, and there were regular chairs with floral patterns that were more reminiscent of my grandmother's living room instead of a doctor's office. I'm sure it was all a conscious effort to help women like me to relax and feel more at ease during an otherwise frightening medical procedure.

As my eyes scanned the room, I noticed a very large photograph of a beautiful pink flower that was mounted on the wall behind my head and off to the right. It was beautiful. I stared at it in awe as the nurse and doctor worked around me, getting things ready. It reminded me of Grandfather's roses. My grandmother loved roses, and my grandfather loved her, so every day he would go outside and "tend to the roses" as he would say, just for her. Looking at that pink flower on the wall and remembering them was the only "medicine" I needed at that time to feel relaxed. There is something about memories, especially those of family, that brings a peace like nothing else can. The music and the flower were exactly what I needed at that time.

The nurse began by rubbing the brown iodine on my chest where the doctor would be working. She then covered me with blue paper, carefully tucking it here and there in order to only expose the lump and surrounding breast area. I watched as the doctor picked up a syringe filled with some kind of numbing medicine and inserted it into my breast several times, depositing a bit of it here and there. He talked to me as he worked, which caused me to feel connected to what was happening. There is nothing worse than having something done to your body and not knowing what is going on, so I was thankful to be a part of it.

To say I was unsettled would be an understatement. It had nothing to do with what was happening at the moment, but rather the results from pathology that could possibly change the rest of my life.

After the nurse was finished, she gave me instructions as to what to watch for, how to care for the small incision, and what to do if I developed a fever, chills, etc. I signed the papers, got dressed, and left. The easy part was over; no pain, no problem.

The hard part, however, was waiting for the lab results. As I left the breast center, I wondered what I could do to occupy my mind and keep my nerves in check until I received the call. My schedule was full for the week with work and a huge paper for one of my classes, and for the first time, I felt good about having so much on my plate. I realized those things were going to be enough to keep me busy and allow my mind to be somewhere else instead of staying fixated on the lump and the results.

A week later the call I'd been expecting came through. I was at work, trying my best to pretend everything was perfect and I wasn't waiting on the call that could break me. We weren't allowed to carry our phones onto the sales floor, so I'd left it under the register, and occasionally I would check it. I just happened to be checking to see if anyone had called when it rang in my hand. I swiped right and answered as fast as I could.

"Ms. Adams? I'm calling from the breast center, and I wanted to let you know that your results are negative."

"Negative?" I repeated. "What does that mean?"

At that point in my journey, I had no idea if negative was a good thing or a bad thing. I mean, the word itself gives off a negative connotation. So how was I supposed to know that negative actually meant good in this situation?

"That means that the fluid is benign, not cancerous," she replied.

"Oh, thank God!" I said, as I let out a huge sigh of relief

and thanked her repeatedly. After hanging up, I texted my son with the good news, and then I shared it with my sister and every friend who had been praying for me.

Life was good, right? I had just been given the best news I could possibly have gotten. Except, remember the little gnawing feeling in my gut? Well, it never left.

I told myself day after day that it was only my imagination. Nothing was wrong, and they had the results to prove it. I felt like a hypochondriac, as if I was trying to make something out of nothing. But I wasn't. I knew what the results were inaccurate—I felt it inside of me—but I had to let it go and believe the ones who held the degrees and who knew better than I did. After all, the results were negative!

Life went on, and I continued working five days a week and going to school. The stress was enough to make me want to pull out my hair at times, but I realized just how blessed of a person I was and how my life could have turned out very differently. I loved my job and my coworkers, and we had a great time laughing and having fun every day. I mean, who wouldn't have a great time working at a giant playground? I was living a great life. I was free of any troubles and able to do what I wanted, but the feeling of having cancer never left me. Actually, it was more than a feeling. It was a knowing instinct. It is hard to explain it to anyone on the outside, but those who have experienced it will agree. There is something that lurks in your spirit, telling you what's wrong and that you need to have it taken care of. I heard Oprah Winfrey say to the effect that God gives us little hints when He wants to get our attention. She said that He will whisper the first time, give you a nudge the second time, and hit you with a brick the last time. I feel that's what He was doing with me. He was "speaking" to me. No, not audibly, but He was letting me know in my spirit that I had a major problem that needed addressed. Some people call that intuition, but I call it discernment.

In Christian contexts, discernment is the ability to obtain spiritual guidance and understanding. I believe when we seek God in any given situation, He will provide guidance and resolution. That is what I was doing regarding the lump. I had been praying for God to show me what was wrong, and He was! He had placed upon my heart the urgency and concern for my health, and I was doing my part of having it checked but each time. It came back benign, so I had carried on with living, trying to forget about it, but it never left me, knowing what I knew deep in my spirit never left me.

By now, you are probably getting tired of reading about the "gnawing feeling." Believe me, I got tired of it too. I began to wonder if *I* was making myself sick. Every time my breast ached or felt sore, I felt like *I* was causing it to happen because I was convinced there was more to it. So I tried even harder to ignore the problem. I pushed the thoughts out of my mind as soon as they entered it. I prayed that God would help me to have power over my mind. I recited the Bible verse found in 2 Timothy 1:7: "God hath not given us a spirit of fear; but of power, and of love, and of a sound mind." (KJV) I stood on His promises that I had control of what came into my mind, and I refused to let the enemy bring something on me that wasn't there. I mean, the lab results showed no cancer, right? So I *needed* to put it out of my mind and live my life. It was imperative that I do so in order to maintain my sanity.

Fast forward to January 2019. The lump was back. And it was bigger. This time it had grown to the size of a tangerine, and it was sore to the touch. Again, I called the breast center, who in turn called my doctor, who in turn sent a referral, so I could have another aspiration performed.

I went through the same process, in the same room.

CANCER, GOD, AND ME

Same music, same picture, same nurse, different doctor. He was as nice as the first doctor and assured me it was probably just a fluid-filled cyst and everything would be okay.

And once more, after about a week, it came back benign, and I felt relived again ... for a while.

I'll spare you the repetitive details of the next four times I had the lump drained, as I finally came to call it. Each time it would get bigger, and each time it hurt more and more.

By the last time it was drained, November 2019, it was so large the doctor pulled off almost a liter of fluid. At that appointment, it was a different doctor who did the procedure. It was still the same place, same room, and same nurse, but thank God it was a new doctor. By that time I had already "accepted" the fact that I had cancer, but no one was finding it, I was angry that they weren't doing more to help me. But what was I to do? I mean, *they* are the medical professionals who have knowledge I don't possess. *They* are the ones we trust with our lives, and if they are telling me it isn't cancer, then who am I to argue? Right? I was in such a state that I didn't know what to do except follow their lead.

I watched the doctor as he looked over my chart and flipped back to the previous pages of notes and aspirations I had already endured. He told me he was concerned about my having to come in so often to have it drained. He thought there might be more to it and suggested I see a surgeon. Finally! There was someone willing to get to the root of it all instead of just having me come back every six to eight weeks and collect $1,667.00. Yes, that's right. It cost that much every single time I had an aspiration done. I had insurance, but I still had to pay copays and twenty percent of each procedure. The last one I had done was without insurance, and I ended up getting the bill for the full amount.

I listened carefully as he discussed with the nurse the specific information that needed to be detailed on the referral, and I knew my life was about to take a turn for which I might not be ready. Remember, I had already suspected I had cancer, but with doctor after doctor telling me the pathology report was negative, I had my hopes up that I was okay. It was easier to let it all go and trust what they told me. It did bring some sense of peace, even though looking back I realize it was denial that I was experiencing. Not wanting to find out you have cancer is a much easier mindset to have than the one that presents itself after learning the terrible news. I think it's the entire reason I didn't go for a second opinion, or a third one. I had my life all planned out, and cancer didn't fit anywhere, so if the doctor was saying I was okay, then I would accept it and go on.

CANCER, GOD, AND ME

Two

The Surgeon I Never Saw

"Be careful for nothing, but in everything by prayer and supplication with thanksgiving, let your requests be made known to God."
- Philippians 4:6

Sometime in late November 2019, I got a call from a kind receptionist who ended up playing a very pivotal role in my journey.

"Good morning, could I speak with Christy Adams?" she spoke softly.

"This is Christy," I replied.

"My name is Sally, and I'm calling to set up your appointment to see Dr. C. We were sent a referral from the breast center regarding a recurring cyst in the right breast." My heart began to beat rapidly as she explained the reason for her call.

This is real. This is happening, was all I could think as I tried to listen to her ask the dates I was available and give me a time to be there. I felt sick and started to sweat. After a few seconds, I summoned up the courage to agree to be there the next week at some time I cannot even remember now. She thanked me politely and said, "I'll see you then," before she hung up. My stomach was quickly moving from feeling queasy to a full-on vomit. But I gained my composure and went back to my statistics homework.

The week passed quickly, and before I realized, it was time for my appointment. I was nervous and scared. I knew what the surgeon was going to find because the lump was huge and noticeably getting bigger by the day. After the previous doctor had pulled off the one liter of fluid, it began to fill up that evening and by the next morning, it was bigger than it had ever been.

I watched it and took pictures as it grew as fear consumed me. Each time I took a shower and stood in front of the mirror, it turned my stomach. Each time I changed clothes I couldn't help but to examine it in all its grandeur. The thing was huge, and it seemed to have not only taken over my breast but my mind and heart as well. So it was a good thing I had the appointment with the surgeon, right? Yes, it was good, but I didn't go. I couldn't. I couldn't bring myself to face what I already knew. I didn't want to *know*. I thought maybe I was just overreacting and letting my mind run away with me, but if I heard it from the doctor, then it would be real. I didn't call to reschedule, nor did I call to cancel. I know, I know, it's a terrible thing to do, and normally I would never do that to a doctor's office, but I was being led by my emotions and not my rational thought process. This, my friend, is denial at its finest.

The next day, Sally called to ask me if I was aware that I had missed my appointment, and I told her yes. I apologized for not calling and said I felt horrible because I had worked for doctors before and we didn't like it when patients just didn't show up with no calls to cancel. She told me it was okay and didn't ask any questions; she simply found another spot on the calendar and told me she'd see me the following week. I agreed and hung up. I honestly did have intentions on going the next time. I mean, I knew it was the most important appointment I would ever have, and so I summoned up the courage to go.

The night before the appointment I didn't sleep a wink. No matter what I did, I couldn't get my eyes to close and find sweet slumber. I tossed and turned so much so my hips were hurting as if my bed was concrete. I got up and scrolled through social media, grabbed some chips, and played a game on my phone just to pass the time. Occasionally, I felt the lump and thought about how maybe if I prayed hard enough, God would take it away. I was familiar with the verse Mark 11:23 that says, "For verily I say unto you, that whosoever shall say unto this mountain, be thou removed, and be thou cast into the sea, and shall not doubt in his heart, but shall believe those things which he saith shall come to pass, he shall have whatsoever he saith." (KJV) Well, that night, I did just that. I prayed and prayed and prayed. And when I was done praying, I prayed some more for good measure. After a few hours, I finally fell asleep from exhaustion. My body had to get some rest, even if it was only going to be half an hour.

The next morning, I got up and you guessed it—I missed my appointment once again. I had made up my mind I was going to trust God to take it all away, but that isn't how God works. I have seen Him move through medicine and doctors. I'm not saying that miracles don't happen, but sometimes miracles come in the form of chemo, surgery, and radiation instead of a lightning bolt from the sky.

What I was really doing was trying to convince myself that nothing was wrong. I couldn't face the fact that something foreign had possibly invaded my body and there was nothing I could do about it. It was almost as if "out of sight, out of mind" was the way to go, if that makes sense. I mean, we've all heard the saying "what you don't know won't hurt you". But that was not the answer for me or any way for me to live when it came to my health. Even though I knew instinctively and had known for some time, I still didn't want to find out from an actual surgeon who would know with certainty. And so the easiest thing was to just ignore it altogether, hence denial, and hence the use of Scripture taken completely out of context.

Denial is the action of declaring something is not true or the refusal to accept a truth. In the world of psychology, it is known as coping or a defense mechanism a person resorts to when she cannot accept what is being experienced. I am a psychology major working on my master's degree, and I look back and wonder how I did not see this in myself at the time. I mean, there was so much evidence with the ever-growing lump, the drainage, the aspirations, and oh yeah, the intuition. But even I, as a student of psychology, knowing all that I know about how the mind works, was able to allow myself to go into denial. As I stated earlier, it was just easier.

This stage happens when one first gets her diagnosis of breast cancer, but you see, I was ahead of the game. I had not been diagnosed with anything yet except a fluid-filled cyst. Remember, I told you I plowed through the five stages of grief? Well, there is the proof. I was in denial before I ever knew anything was wrong, and I would continue this pattern for a while.

I'm a firm believer in speaking the Word of God over our lives, ourselves, our children, finances, homes, and families. I believe we have the power through the Holy Spirit and God's Word to speak blessings into our lives—or curses. Proverbs 18:21 states, "Death and life are in the power of the tongue and they that love it shall eat the fruit thereof." (KJV) We can build others up or tear them down. We can build ourselves up or tear ourselves down. I wrote a devotional titled "Speak Life: Declaring God's Word Over Your Day," so I know the importance of speaking life over ourselves.

I also know the importance of taking every verse in Scripture and using it in the context it was meant. We cannot distort the Word of God to fit our agendas and expect our prayers to be answered the way we want them to be simply because we are quoting His Word. No, we must get to the heart of the verse and seek out the true meaning of it before we go tossing it out like it's some sort of magic dust that will make life's troubles disappear.

Is it good that I quoted Mark 11:23? Yes, but I also know there is another verse in the Bible where we are told that if we ask amiss, we will not receive that for which we have prayed. James 4:3 tells us, "Ye ask and receive not because ye ask amiss, that ye may consume it upon your lusts." (KJV) James was telling the people that when they asked for what they wanted, they were doing so in an effort to manipulate God instead of trusting Him for His perfect will in their lives.

Well, I was only wanting God to heal me immediately instead of walking the path He had laid out for me.

Is it wrong to ask to be healed? No, it's not. God wants to heal us. Look at all the times in His Word when He healed people. But He wants us to come to Him and say, "Not my will, but thy will be done." When we can get to that place with God and put His plans for our lives first, *then* we will see Him work on our behalf.

What does it take to get there? Complete trust in Him and knowing His ways, His thoughts, and His plans for us are above ours.

CANCER, GOD, AND ME

Three

Hello, December!
(Is it Christmas yet?)

"Heal me, O Lord, and I shall be healed."
- Jeremiah 17:4

It was December, a time of joy and happiness. A time to put up the tree, buy gifts, and be jolly. A time to celebrate with family and friends and forget about life's worries. And I was going to do exactly that. I wasn't going to agonize about the already extremely large lump in my breast that was increasing in size with each passing day. No! I was going to keep praying for God to take it away and live my life.

You know, God *is* a miracle worker. He *is* willing to heal us and make us whole. It is His will that we are well.

His Word has many verses of Jesus telling people to only believe and be made whole. Luke 8:50 is a perfect example of Him saying, "Only believe."

The daughter of the ruler of the synagogue was very ill, and he went to see Jesus because he knew just one touch from Him could heal her. But as he was getting ready to ask Him to come, one of his servants told him that she was already dead and not to trouble Jesus. When Jesus heard, He told the father of the girl, "Fear not: only believe and she shall be made whole." (KJV) And just before that incident, the woman with the issue of blood had touched the hem of his garment and was made whole because she believed He could heal her.

Well, I was doing just that. I was believing for my miracle. I was asking for Him to take it all away and let me keep living my life as I had been.

You see, I have always hated change. Everything has to remain the same. I must stay on a schedule to feel normalcy in my life. I'm very disciplined when it comes to work, college, and keeping things running as planned every day. So this lump, cyst, or whatever I was dealing with was causing my life to become messy. Having to deal with it was causing me to not be "on track," as I so often referred to my inflexible schedule. I wanted life to be as I wanted it: church, school, work, home. Nothing more, nothing less. I had my plans, and I wanted it to remain the same. Yet, I was praying every day that God would use me to be a great witness for Him. I was already telling everyone who came through my store at Dollywood about Jesus, and I was posting His goodness on social media. But I knew there was more I could be doing for Him. Should be doing more. I felt that He could use me to reach more people than I had already, and I wanted Him to do it. "Just use me, Lord," I would say every night when I prayed. He was trying, but I was resisting. I didn't know it at the time, though. God was going to place me on the path I was destined to end up on and use it for His glory. I don't know if I couldn't see that or if I didn't want to see it because I kept praying for Him to heal me, so I wouldn't have to go through what I perceived was waiting for me.

I knew He would heal me if I prayed hard enough and believed. Except, He didn't.

Now, here is the conundrum. I was asking and believing, just like He had said, but I wasn't getting better. The lump was still there. With each passing day and each prayer that I prayed, the problem remained.

I began to question myself. Am I not praying enough? Do I not have enough faith? Am I not saying the right words? I was beginning to question myself and my faith in God. I never questioned Him, only myself.

All my life, I had always had faith in God. Do not ask me how because I wasn't raised in a church-going family. I went when I was very young because my grandfather was an Apostolic preacher, but he died when I was eight-years-old, and so our days of going to church were pretty much over. My other grandparents had raised me, and they did not attend church, ever. I did, however, begin attending a church when I was about seventeen or eighteen-years-old, and I developed a close relationship with God and began to trust Him in a way I had never known possible. And so, my deep faith in God began. My friends at that church always told me they admired me because I was able to believe when no one else did. I had a child-like faith in Him that I cannot explain to this day. I just knew that God told us in His Word to trust Him, and I did. I always did and always will.

So why wasn't He taking away the lump? If my faith in Him was so big, and I knew His Word, why wasn't He healing me? Well, that's a tough question to answer. I still don't know if I have the right answer or not, but I will tell you how I feel about it. Please note that before you read this, it is only my experience, and I do not speak for everyone. We all must find our own way in life and navigate our own relationships with God. I can tell you my experience, but in the end, it is each person's journey to walk with God.

You see, at the time, I did not have the understanding that if we want to be used by Him, then we must turn over our will to Him. We must turn our desires for our lives to what He desires for us. And we must realize that if we are going to be witnesses of His goodness, then we have to have something to witness about. We must first have a test before we have a testimony.

Now, back to the giant lump. December was passing by, and Sally was insistent on calling me once a week. I told her I would get back to her when I had my insurance lined out. During the time between not going to see the surgeon and mid-December, I had lost my health insurance due to a mix up in auto-billing.

Was that just another defense mechanism of coping by denial? Maybe. I mean, I was using it as my reason to not go and get checked. But Sally was offering to put me on a payment plan, give me a hefty discount, and even help me to get insurance *if* it turned out to be breast cancer.

That all sounded good, but I still refused to go see the

surgeon. I told her I would let her know when I could come in, and we could set up the appointment then. She agreed, and I went on about my life of trying to ignore the lump and Sally's calls.

Toward the middle of December, my breast with the lump began to have a discharge from the nipple. It was small at first, just a spot or two during the day. But at night, when I went to bed, it was worse.

The first time it happened, I woke up in the middle of the night and my pajama top was soaked—I felt wetness on my chest, arm, all around me. I wondered if I had reached for my bottle of water on the nightstand in my sleep and maybe spilled a little of it. I have been known to sleepwalk, and so anything was possible. After sitting up and turning on the lamp, I saw my sheet was wet as well.

"What's going on?" I wondered aloud, as if there was anyone there to answer me. In my confusion, I got up and went to the bathroom to investigate the situation. I pulled off my wet top and noticed my breast was covered in a yellowish discharge, mixed with blood. My shirt was covered in the mysterious substance as well. My heart sank. And at that very moment, I was shaken to my core. A fear deeper than I had felt before gripped my heart and spirit, and I knew that something horrific was indeed going on. I grabbed my phone and took pictures in case the doctor needed to see them. I'm glad I did because I can now use them to educate women on what breast cancer looks like.

I considered calling Sally and getting an appointment, but I was paralyzed by the outcome that I feared awaited me. I know that sounds crazy, but at that point, I was *convinced* I had cancer, but yet I was too afraid of hearing the words. There was no more telling myself, "Oh, put those thoughts out of your mind. Take control of your thoughts." No, now I knew deep in my heart that simply taking control of my thoughts wasn't going to be enough to change any of what was happening.

So I tried to ignore it. Do not ask me how that makes the situation any better because it doesn't, but during the denial phase, you feel as if ignoring the problem means it isn't there and does not exist.

Anna Freud, daughter of famed psychoanalyst Sigmund Freud, first developed the idea of denial. She proposed that if a situation was too much for a person to handle emotionally and mentally, then the individual simply refused to experience it.

That was exactly what I was doing. I was experiencing denial before I ever had the first doctor's appointment.

December ended and January began. It was a new year,

CANCER, GOD, AND ME

2020, and things were going to be great. I had left Dollywood, and begun a new job, one where I could travel all year going to different conferences all over the country. One where I could learn, grow, and move up eventually. Things were going great for me. I was still in college working on my degree, and I was happy with everything in my life ... except the lump. It was still there and bigger than ever. It had actually appeared to have split into two lumps. I don't know if it had literally split or what, but in my pictures, it looks as if there are two there. By that time, it had turned a very dark purple or black color, kind of like a bruise does. I was still having the discharge every night, but now it had a *lot* of blood coming out of it.

The horror I experienced the first time I saw blood was unimaginable if you've never been through it. We know when we see blood coming out of any place in our bodies, it's not good. So when I saw it literally coming out of my nipple, I was convinced I was going to die of breast cancer.

One would think being in such a state as I was, blood, discharge, huge lump, that I would call the doctor immediately and demand to be seen. But no, I didn't. I tried to go on and ignore it, as crazy as that sounds. I didn't even call the doctor. I was still trying to deny what was apparent to me.

CHRISTY ADAMS

Every night I would put a washcloth in my bra and let it soak up the blood and discharge. I would get up several times during the night and put in a fresh, clean cloth when the other had gotten too wet. During the day, I filled my bra cup with toilet paper to soak up the gunk flowing from my poor breast.

One day, while I was in the ladies' room at work, I unfurled about twenty squares of toilet paper and placed it in my bra, careful not to touch the excruciatingly tender lump. I laughed as my mind went back to when I was a ten-year-old girl stuffing my bra with my little sister. Looking back, I know it was another coping mechanism. After all, the old saying goes, laughter is the best medicine.

The humor wore off quickly, though, as I started using pantyliners in my bra to keep the discharge from seeping through and onto my shirt each day. At night, I had switched from washcloths to hand towels. I have pictures of all of it: the washcloths, the hand towels, the bloody pajamas. I wanted to document what was going on. I'm glad I did. Now I can show others and make them aware of what can happen to your body when you do not take care of yourself and ignore all the warning signs.

I told a friend one day, actually, I have used this as my analysis of the situation with many people, and now I will share it with you. I said that when we have something like that happening in our bodies and God is trying to help us, He will use things to get our attention. The little hard lump that I first found was God's way of saying, "Hey, get this checked." I did, and they ruled it not cancerous. God let it come back and again said, "Hey, it's back, get it checked." Again, I did, and it was nothing. You see, God knew the cancer was there, and He was trying to get me and the doctors to find it, but they weren't looking deeply enough into it. They were simply taking off the fluid without trying to find the root cause of the problem. That would come later, and I will explain how that happened in the next chapter. But God kept giving me those little nudges to get checked. And the last doctor who wanted to send me to the surgeon was the one who listened to God's nudge. He set it up, but I was the one who refused. So what did God do? He allowed it to get bigger so that I would do something, but I didn't. Then He allowed it to bleed so that I would finally listen to Him. God is good like that. He will go to the end with us, but we have to listen and obey what He is telling us. I could have continued to ignore it and let it go until it killed me. I was stage three, grade 3

when it was found, and it was on my chest wall, so that was bad enough. All I can say is that my denial ran so deeply that I chose to ignore everything my body and mind were telling me.

After my diagnosis, I was told that when I first found the tiny, jellybean-sized lump, the cancer had probably already been there at least two-to-five years. After doing research to see if that was true, I found an article that made me question things that had been happening for years, but I hadn't given them a second thought. Those things included itching on my breast, swollen feet and ankles, sore breasts, etc., all of which can be indicators of breast cancer (although not always).

According to a study done by Nakashima, K., Uematsu, T., Takahashi, K. et al, titled, *Does Breast Cancer Growth Rate Really Depend on Tumor Subtype?* "It is likely that tumors began a minimum of five years before detection." [1]

One day, while I was at work, I happened to be on my lunch break when Sally called, again. I hadn't heard from her in a couple of weeks, and so I answered, knowing what she wanted. She said I had been on her mind, and she had been praying for me and asked how I was doing. I explained what was going on, and she all but begged me to come in for an appointment. She was very concerned for me at that point, and I could hear the uneasiness in her voice. After much going back and forth about not having insurance and not wanting a big bill, I finally said okay, partly to get it over with and partly because I knew I truly needed to go.

I told my boss I needed a couple of hours off one morning the following week. She told me to write it on the whiteboard, and that was that. As I sat down at my desk, I felt a little relieved that I was finally going to find out what was going on with my poor, swollen, misshapen, discolored breast.

Four

My Journey Begins

"Trust in the Lord with all thine heart and lean not unto thine own understanding."

- Proverbs 3:5

The day I dreaded had arrived. It was the morning of my appointment with the surgeon. I had been told by the doctor at the breast center that the surgeon would look at it and probably do a lumpectomy to remove the cyst so I would not have to have it drained anymore. Simple, right? I thought so too. So I arrived at the front desk, looked through the glass and introduced myself to Sally, the sweet lady who hadn't given up on me. I'm more grateful to her than she will ever know. Incidentally, Sally left that office to take a job at another location after my first appointment. When I went back a couple of weeks later, she was gone. I was sad because I wanted to express my gratitude to her for helping me have the courage to come in. I sometimes think about how I almost missed that opportunity. Sally was leaving, and she knew it, but I didn't. What if I had waited a while longer? Would the new receptionist have called repeatedly as Sally had? I doubt it. She didn't even seem to know how to check me in when I did go back, so I can't really imagine she would have put as much effort into getting someone to come in who clearly didn't seem interested in saving her own life. No, I was blessed with Sally. She will forever be an angel to me.

Within a couple of minutes, I heard my name called, and I looked up to see a younger nurse standing in the doorway. She introduced herself, weighed me, and took me to the exam room. I was told to take off my shirt and bra and slip into the designer paper cape in the boring shade of what I refer to as blah blue, ha ha. I did as she asked and parked my bottom on the exam table. As I looked around the room, I felt a chill in the air. I know they have to keep those places cool to combat germs, but this was downright cold. I dreaded opening my cape for fear the doctor would see that I was super cold. But however thin the paper, it was at least keeping me from freezing too much. I hate exam rooms with all of their sterility. It's just me on the table, looking around at the cabinets, dying to peek inside but knowing I'll get caught as soon as I open the first door. Pretty much all there is to do is wait on the table, read, and reread each and every poster on the walls until you hear the voice of either a nurse or the doctor. I'd much rather wait outside in the reception area because at least out there I can talk to others. But in that room, I was left alone with my thoughts and fears, and I was growing more afraid with each passing minute.

As I continued to wait, I began to think about how he was going to tell me the worst news I could ever hear, and then I told myself it was nothing, and I was overthinking the whole situation. I told myself I was okay because every pathology report had come back benign, and I had nothing to worry about except allowing my imagination to run wild with my thoughts. I kept bouncing back and forth in my mind from fear to faith, faith to fear. I mean, at that point, I knew without actually knowing.

Plastered on the wall in front of me, I saw a sign that said, "Cell phones are not allowed in the exam room." There went my one item of comfort to take my mind off of the impending news that weighed heavily on my shoulders. I caught myself nervously tapping my foot against the bottom of the table as I waited for what seemed to be an eternity. I read every poster twice and looked at some small model of an artery or some internal body part that was sitting next to the sink.

After a few minutes more, I heard a gentle knock, and then the door opened. In walked this gorgeous man who was apparently the surgeon. *Whoa!!* How could he be the doctor? He was so handsome. He looked like an actor from one of the television shows where the doctors are all hot and the nurses are beautiful.

"Hello, I'm Dr. C," he said as he extended his hand to shake mine.

"Hi," I said and blushed, I'm sure.

All I could do was stare at this beautiful man in front of me with his salt and pepper hair and perfect teeth. *Come on, Christy,* I thought to myself as I tried to concentrate on his words. I mean, after all, I was a fifty-one-year-old woman, and he was my doctor. Y'all, I am telling you if you ever saw him, you would know what I'm talking about. This man belongs in an ad for cologne or on a billboard in Times Square.

After he took a look at what by this time was a *very* large lump, he explained it was probably just a cyst and he would simply do the lumpectomy, and I would be good to go. He said that by doing surgery, he would remove the entire sac so the cyst couldn't fill up again, and that would be that. From his lips to God's ears, right! I was so happy and immensely relieved. I thanked him with a huge smile, got dressed, and stopped at the scheduler's office to arrange the surgery.

Trish, the scheduling nurse, became my lifeline that day. If you have ever had cancer or any type of horrific illness, then you know what I'm talking about when I say those who care for you become more than just doctors and nurses; they become your superheroes, in a sense. You never look at them the same way you did before. They become a source of comfort in an unknown territory. They have the answers you're searching for and the ability to make you feel safe when everything is falling apart. I will never be able to express my gratitude for those who have cared for me over the past year and a half.

After being scheduled, I left and began to dread the surgery itself. I've been afraid of being put to sleep ever since my mom passed away from a heart catherization in 2005. I had gallbladder removal surgery in 2011 and almost died just after the procedure due to receiving too much valium in the operating room, so that added to my fear of being put to sleep as well. I knew I had no choice, and so I continued telling myself I would be okay. It was a simple surgery to remove the cyst and then life would be back to normal.

Surgery day came, and I reluctantly went in with my son in tow. Arriving early had always been something I was good at because when I got my first job at seventeen, my grandpa told me, "It's better to be thirty minutes early than one minute late." That has stuck with me all of my life. And so, if you ever have an appointment with me or are planning to go anywhere with me, you know that I show up early.

The planned procedure was supposed to be outpatient and expected to take about an hour. Being put under anesthesia was one of the things I feared the most. I was so nervous by the time I had signed in and was shown to my room that my legs were shaking just as much as my hands were. I had my son step out for a moment so I could put on the surgery patient uniform—ugly blue gown with some type of little print, yellow slip-resistant socks, and flimsy blue cap. Once I was back in bed, he came back in and proceeded to try to comfort me with jokes. I knew what he was doing, and I realized he needed to tell the jokes as much for himself as for me. He was afraid of what was going to happen. My son has never been one to show emotion very much. He gets that from his father. Both are quiet human beings who don't really get upset much or cry, but I could tell that on this day, Josh was nervous and scared. So I let him tell me all the corny jokes he wanted to so he could comfort himself as well as me. After all, the Bible tells us in Proverbs that a merry heart does good like medicine.

Slowly, nurses made their way in and out, asking me questions, taking my vital signs, and putting in the IV. The anesthesiologist came in and talked to me about his role in the procedure, and I made him promise to sit with me and not leave me. He smiled and said that is what he does with all of his patients. I knew that, but just hearing him say it somehow brought me extra comfort. I asked to be knocked out in the room before even moving me because I knew if I saw the operating room, I would have been more afraid. So the anesthesiologist gave me something in my IV, and about three seconds later I was out.

I don't remember anything after that until I got back to

my room where my son was waiting for me. I don't even remember being in recovery. I've never been good with anesthesia, and it takes me a long time to come out of it.

The bright spot of the whole thing was a video my son made where he was asking me questions about my name, the date, etc., and I was too groggy to even talk. I don't even remember the doctor coming in to talk to me afterward. I'm not even sure he did.

I was released a short while later, and Josh drove me home, put me to bed, and let me sleep off the strong meds.

The doctor had told me he would send the tissue off to pathology to be on the safe side and check it once more, so I tried my best to not be anxious while I waited for the results.

Five

The Call

"For I the Lord thy God will hold thy right hand, saying unto thee, Fear not; I will help thee."
- Isaiah 41:13

Thursday, February 13th, 2020. Nothing to do, nowhere in particular to be for me that day, so why not sleep late? It was going to be a beautiful day with sunshine and a high of sixty-one degrees, and I'd planned to drive out to the lake later in the afternoon. I had already been laid off work when I had the lumpectomy, and so I was trying to catch up on some rest. Yes, you read that correctly. My boss actually laid me off the day I told her about what was going on with my health. But that's okay. I think everyone was laid off at the end of the month anyway because of Covid, so it was bound to happen one way or the other.

It was 8:05 a.m., the day I got the call that determined what the rest of my life looked like; not just the rest of my day, but the rest of my actual life.

I heard that familiar ringtone of Santa on the Rooftop (yep, I use it year-round. Remember, I told you that I don't like change). I sat up and looked at my phone to see Dr. C's office number. I wondered if it was Trish calling to tell me the results had come back benign like all the aspirations had, or if she had much worse news to relay.

"Hello," I said after I put the phone to my ear.

"Ms. Adams, this is Dr. C. I have your pathology results."

Dr. C? Why is he calling me? I wondered. Normally, it was a nurse who called with test results. I knew right then it wasn't going to be good.

I took a deep breath and slowly exhaled as I braced myself for what I was about to hear. I didn't say anything. I just gripped the phone tighter.

"I'm sorry to have to tell you the pathology results came back, and it shows that you do have breast cancer."

I sat there, numb. I couldn't speak. All I could hear was the humming of my box fan that I use every night to help me sleep. Judging by the way he continued after my pause, I'm sure he probably knew I was in a state of shock at what I had just heard.

"When I removed the cyst, I saw some suspicious tissue behind it, and I took some of that as well. The cyst itself was nothing but a benign, fluid-filled cyst like we had suspected. But you do have breast cancer, and it was tucked away and hiding behind the cyst against the chest wall."

The only thing I could say was, "Okay." I was at a complete loss for any words that made sense. It was as if I had forgotten the English language.

"The type of cancer you have is triple negative invasive ductal carcinoma."

I had never heard of any of those words before and didn't know what any of it meant. It honestly sounded as if he had just spoken a foreign language to me, and I had to figure it all out.

He went on to explain he was going to a breast conference where he would meet with the oncologist, radiation doctor, and others on a panel to discuss my case along with other cases he had found in his other patients. Apparently, this conference is something they do every week or so. He informed me Trish would set up an appointment to come in the following week, and we would go from there.

He then asked if I had any questions, and I told him no. Even though there were a million things swirling in my mind at that moment, I realized I wouldn't be able to put together enough words to form a question to ask him even if I wanted to.

But somehow, after a few seconds, I managed to summon up the courage to speak. "I've felt it inside of me for quite a while now. Don't ask me how, but I knew it was cancer," I said in a solemn voice with zero emotion.

Like I said, I was numb.

He told me most of his patients said the same thing. That somehow, they just know.

I thanked him for all he had done and said goodbye. He transferred me to Trish, who let me know that she was sorry for my news and scheduled my appointment to go in the following week.

Now what?

How would I tell Josh I have cancer? How could I come to terms with the one thing I feared the absolute most in life, let alone break the horrible news to my son?

How would I tell my sister, my friends? What was I going to do about work? I mean, I had lost my other job, but I had planned on applying somewhere else. I couldn't be employed. I mean, everyone needs income to survive! What was I going to do now?

I put the phone down beside me, laid back on my bed, and stared at the ceiling for a while. Still unable to cry, I felt as if someone had drained me of every feeling I had ever felt in my life. I had *always* been an emotional person. Just ask anyone who had ever watched a sad movie with me, I was the first one (and usually the only one) to cry. Every service at church evoked some type of tear-filled snot-fest from of me. And any driver who was on my tail always got an angry brake check from me while I was traveling. So, yes, I was one who was always in touch with my emotions ... until that day. Instead of being reduced to a sobbing mess on the floor, I was calm. And empty.

Josh was working from home and I knew it was almost time for him to clock in, so I didn't want to just barge in and lay something this heavy on him right before he had to deal with clients. I felt that would have been reckless on my part as his mother. And my sister was probably still in bed (she's not an early riser) and the last thing I wanted to do was wake her with the news that her only sibling was possibly going to die. So, I took a deep breath and called my friend, Joyce. She is twenty years older than I am and has always been like my second mother to me. I wanted her to know so that she could begin praying for me right away. This was not something I could face alone. I knew I was going to need God to step in and help me.

When she answered, I began to cry. It was as if hearing someone else's voice brought it all to the surface. The emotions that had refused to rear their ugly head for the past hour came forth like a tsunami. I told her the doctor had called, and I tried my best to recite everything he had told me. I knew it was to no avail because I barely heard anything he had said while I was on the phone with him. I told her I had cancer and I would know more the next week after my appointment with him. I was sobbing, and she began to cry too. She tried her best to comfort me as she told me we would just have to start praying hard for God to heal me. You see, in 2015, Joyce had lost her young daughter-in-law to lung cancer. She was the mother of two of Joyce's grandchildren, and I'm sure hearing my devasting news brought to the surface the heartache Joyce had felt when her daughter-in-law died.

We cried together for a bit before we hung up so that I could tell Josh. After hanging up with her I tried my best to find the strength to break this news to my only child. I prayed and asked God to give me the words to tell Josh without falling apart. I wanted to be strong for *him*. I was afraid if he saw me in a mess, then he would follow suit, and we would both be in trouble. No, we needed to be strong for each other.

I calmed myself and went to his office door. When I didn't hear him talking I realized that he must be on his first break of the day. Like I said, laying all of that at his feet soon after he began his workday may not have been the best thing for me to do, but I didn't want him to hear me talking to anyone else before he found out. I wanted him to know even before my sister. So, at that moment, right or wrong, I told him. Looking back, maybe I should have kept it to myself until he clocked out at the end of the day. Maybe it was selfish of me to tell when he had to go right back to work. If I could do it all over again, I would definitely have waited. But hindsight is 20/20 and we can't fix our mistakes.

I sat down and looked up at him. I'm pretty sure he knew before I even said a word. It breaks my heart to remember the look of sadness and overwhelming fear in his eyes as I explained what Dr. C. had told me. He started crying and wrapped his arms around me tightly. My heart broke as I saw tears streaming down his face, knowing there was nothing I could do about it. When he was little and he cried, I would pick him up, hug him close to me, and within minutes he would calm down. But that day, no number of hugs could take away the pain he felt.

Josh and I have a close relationship. A very special

bond. He's a momma's boy in every good way and he's proud of that fact. He had been with me through an abusive relationship with an ex-boyfriend and the time we were homeless shortly after I left the relationship. He refused to leave me during that time and go stay with his father, where he would've had a warm home to live in. He has chosen to stick with me through the toughest times in our lives, and I knew this time would be no different. I was certain I could count on my son to have strength when I had none. But still, I hated placing something so heavy at his feet. My son had been through enough, and there I was telling him he was about to go through another terrible thing in his life. But I had no choice. The cancer was there, and it had to be faced head-on, by both of us.

We hugged and cried, and I told him I was going to fight with everything in me to beat it. I was trying to convince him of something of which I wasn't even sure myself. It must have worked because he smiled, hugged me once more, and proceeded to take his chair and clock in. Or maybe he was just trying to convince me he was okay and could handle the bad news. Either way, we both were putting on a happy face—or as happy as we could at the time—for each other. We agreed that day we would be the strength each other needed when we were down.

I went back into my bedroom and laid down, thinking maybe I could drift into sleep and forget about the horrific, life-altering news I had just been given. No such luck. It was way too heavy to allow me to rest, so I just laid there. My little dog, Abby, hopped up on the bed and walked over to me. She carefully laid down on my stomach and stared into my eyes. It was as if she knew I had just found out what *she* had known all along. I say that because Abby is part Dachshund and part Pomeranian. She has always been like a bloodhound, able to sniff out things that are hidden. I can bring a new toy to her or a new rawhide and hide it in the corner of a closet without her even seeing it beforehand, and she will sniff it out until she finds it. I have always said she should've been a police dog if she could've and sniffed out drugs or criminals.

For several months, Abby had been smelling my chest every time she got near me. She would sniff and then back away. Each time she did it, I knew in my heart what was happening. I realized she could probably smell the cancer. I have heard that some animals can sniff out diseases long before they are ever found. I think my little Abby had known for a long time.

That day seemed to drag on. What felt like a hundred hours was really only a few. I gave my sister time to wake up and then called her and told her the news. She cried, of course, and I tried to comfort her the way I had done with my son a few hours earlier. I told her I was going to fight with everything in me, and we would get through it. I'm not sure she was convinced. My heart broke for her. Just hearing the sobs on the other end of the line made me want to drive to West Virginia and wrap my arms around her and never let go.

My sister is fragile. She hasn't always been that way, though. She used to be so strong and seemed indestructible to me, but the circumstances of life and her own illnesses have worn her down. She was always the tough one I could count on to have my back, no matter what. She was brash and rough, not in a bad way, but in all the ways that were good and protective. But now, with her having lost her sight almost completely to diabetes, the diabetes itself and dealing with depression from having lost our mom several years earlier, she seemed like a mere shell of the person I had once known.

She isn't the same foul-mouthed tough girl who had life by the kahunas and ruled the world. No, now she is weak and frail. I felt so sorry for her the day I told her because I knew losing me would kill her. I'm all she has as far as immediate blood family. I mean, she has my son, of course, but I'm her sister, and we have a bond that no other two relatives share. If you have a sibling, you know what I'm talking about. Sisters are special. Lisa and I have been through hell and back together, and that only strengthens the love we have for each other. We are each other's defenders and guardians. You mess with one, you mess with the other. Heck, she even beat up a woman once who came to my house looking to start trouble with me. When she brazenly said she was there to kick my tail, my sister calmly descended my porch steps and proceeded to beat the living daylights out of her, leaving her with a broken nose and a very bruised ego. At the end, she even had the woman crying and apologizing to her.

But now here was an enemy she couldn't fight for me. This invisible demon was out for my life, and my sister couldn't protect me. This monster was going to cause her more heartache than she deserved. I felt such sadness for her. My sister, my champion, could no longer stand in the gap for me. This time, it was up to me to fight for myself.

CANCER, GOD, AND ME

Six

Now What?

"But as for you, ye thought evil against me; but God meant it unto good."

- Genesis 50:20

It had been a couple of days since my mind had been overloaded to the point of not being able to function normally. There was too much in there for me to try to sort out. It was stuffed with words I wasn't familiar with, and I had no idea what to do with them. They were crammed in there, giving me a headache as they bounced off each other as they fought for space. I had to do something to get those thoughts under control. I had to take back the place in my mind before it caused my head to explode!

It reminds me of when my son does his laundry and

stuffs the washing machine to overload. It's so full I wonder how it all gets wet, much less clean. Once the washing machine fills with water, the clothes usually get unbalanced, and the tub begins to bang the side of the machine until it sounds like it's going to blow apart. As soon as he hears the loud noise, he runs to it, opens the lid, and sorts it all out by evenly spacing the clothes apart so they have enough room to move. I've even seen him take some out and wash them later on.

That's how my mind felt. There was too much stuffed in there for me to function properly. I realized I was going to have to move some things around and even get rid of some of those thoughts that were causing me to not be able to function if I was going to move forward. So I did just that.

One of my favorite places to go here in East Tennessee is Douglas Lake. It's been a place of peace for many years. I don't necessarily have to be out in a boat or swimming to feel tranquility; I can just go sit at the boat dock and stare out onto the water and feel calmness. And that's what I did. I grabbed my car keys and headed to the boat dock.

I live about ten minutes from Walter's Boat Dock. Sometimes during the summer I just go and park my car and watch people fish or ride jet skis. It's very relaxing for me because I'm all by myself with no one else around. I turn off my phone ringer and sit there staring at the lake. Water has always held some type of calming power for me. From my understanding it does that for many others as well. Science explains that when we hear moving water, it triggers a response in our brains that brings out a flood of neurochemicals, which in turn, increases blood flow to the brain and heart. There is a book by marine biologist Wallace J. Nichols called, Blue Mind, that speaks in depth about the benefits of being around water and why we are drawn to it. I know for myself, even as a child, I loved water. We had a very large in-ground swimming pool when I was growing up, and I all but lived in it during the summer months. As soon as Spring arrived, I would aggravate my grandfather relentlessly until he pulled the cover off and "got it ready" as I called it. I wanted to be in the water 24/7. I used to say I should've been born a mermaid instead of a human. I still feel that way.

I sat in my car by the lake and watched as the sun glistened on the water. It was low, of course, because just before winter, they let down the water level so as not to allow the lake to flood after rain and snowstorms. When it's low like that, you can see the beautiful lakebed with tree stumps and branches. Sometimes there will be people out cleaning up the garbage that may have gotten tossed overboard someone's boat. But I have never seen much of that because most people appreciate the beauty of it and take care not to litter.

It was warm for February—sixty degrees—so I rolled down my windows and listened to the stillness. Two men sat quietly in a Jon boat, casting their lines out into the water. Were they really trying to catch fish or escaping life's heartaches for a moment, like I was doing? Perhaps a little of both.

Sitting there in my car, I thought about everything ... the innocent lump that had been hiding the real culprit the whole time; Josh, who was probably more afraid than he would ever admit; my sister, who wouldn't be able to take the death of another family member. I thought about all the people I had loved over the years: friends, family, my ex-husband, and boyfriends who had drifted in and out of my life. I wondered what they would all do when they heard the news. I knew most of them would be devastated by my ailment, but I also realized there were a few, with whom I had parted on bad terms, who would be doing a happy dance. I hate to say that, but it's true. Not every relationship I've had ended with a smile and a handshake. But I couldn't think about them. No, I had to save my energy to fight the demon inside of me.

I put my hand on my chest and felt the area where the lump had been. The scar was still fresh and a little sore, but I was trying to find the enemy. I wanted to know what the cancer felt like. I wanted to know what it looked like. I wanted to see my new adversary, so I would know who I was fighting.

Ever since I was little and I had heard the word cancer, I envisioned a group of ugly green cells that were marching in a huge mass inside the body. It was the ugliest picture I could come up with, and so that's the image I kept in my mind. But now, sitting by the lake, it was as if the cancer had grown legs and had risen up and was looking me right in the eye. *My* cancer was now this formidable beast who was out for my life. I closed my eyes and began to pray. I asked God for strength as I began to walk a journey that I didn't want to walk. I asked Him for comfort, not only for me, but for my family and friends as well. I prayed for courage to face whatever came my way. And I prayed He would help me to use the cancer battle as a testimony of His goodness. That day, at that boat dock, I made up my mind that I was going to use it for good. In Genesis 50:20, the Bible says, "But as for you, ye thought evil against me; but God meant it unto good, to bring it to pass, as it is this day, to save many people alive." (KJV) I thought about how everything *can* have a purpose if we let it; how everything we experience can bring glory to God, even if in the end it doesn't turn out like we want it to, it can still be used to glorify the Kingdom of God. I knew that was what I wanted. I wanted my journey to have a purpose. I remember hearing my own voice as I prayed and said, "God, don't let this cancer be for nothing. Don't let this enemy come in here and take my life for no reason. Use this to build your Kingdom and bring others to you, in Jesus name." And that is exactly what He has done.

Seven

The Plan

"A man's heart deviseth his ways: but the Lord directeth His steps."

- Proverbs 16:9

Those who know me have always known that one of my mantras has invariably been, "Here's the plan." I've said that for the majority of my life. One of my friends finds it amusing that I have a plan for everything that comes my way, and it causes her to laugh every time she hears me say it. But it's just who I've always been as a person. It's probably because of the terrible things I went through as a child, (my dad passing away when I was six-years-old, and then having been sexually abused from nine to eleven-years-old).

Having a plan in place was my way of controlling my life. And it worked for a while ... or maybe I liked to pretend it did. After all, my life has always seemed to be like a runaway train on a downhill track that I never really could control. But just the thought of having a plan seemed to help me feel some semblance of authority over what happened to me each day.

There's a quote by Michael Chabon that states, "Man makes plans, and God laughs." I have to agree. That's not to say God is mocking us. No, rather He is saying, "That is not what *I* have laid out for your life" or "That is not *my* will."

Now, I know there are some who believe in destiny and fate and all that jazz, but I'm one who believes that when we surrender our hearts and *our* will to *God*'s will, then His plan becomes the guiding force of our lives. He will lead us where He wants us to go in order to fulfill the calling which He placed on our lives.

When I gave my heart and life to the Lord, I told Him He could do with me whatever He wanted.

I said, "God, I want your will and purpose for my life."

You see, I was tired of going my own way and always ending up in trouble. I realized my way and my plan were never for my good. Every ... single ... time, I ended up in a mess. But I knew without a doubt God's plans were for my benefit, and so I left it up to Him to take me where He wanted me to go. I also remember telling Him I had spent too many years wasting my time on the foolish desires of my heart, and I finally wanted my life to mean something for Him. Now, having said all of that to Him, who was I to question where He was now leading me? Who was I to say anything or be upset and sad about the path ahead?

The man Job, in the Bible, who suffered more than anyone except Jesus, never opened his mouth to curse God regarding the horrific things that were happening to him. Job had lost everything he had. He lost his children, his land, his animals, his wealth; all without questioning God. He did, however, wish he had never been born in the first place (Job 3:16). His words came from a place of pain, though. Not only the physical anguish he was experiencing, but mental and emotional pain as well. He had lost everything except his life, and I'm sure there was a tremendous amount of grief in his heart. And it worked its way out, and he spoke in haste. After all, the Bible tells us in Matthew 12:34, "Out of the abundance of the heart, the mouth speaks." So Job was only speaking from the pain in his heart.

I made the decision almost immediately that I wasn't going to allow negative speech to come from my mouth regarding my cancer journey. I remember praying and telling God I wanted the diagnosis to be for a purpose. I didn't want to just get cancer and it not be used for good. I wanted my journey to be a positive experience that would bring glory to God.

Yeah, I know. How can cancer be positive? It doesn't really make sense, does it? I wanted something good to come from something terrible. Now, having said all that, does that mean I was always Ms. Sunshine who was leaving rainbows wherever I went? No, I wasn't. There were days I was sad and felt alone. There were days I felt anger. Remember, anger is one of the stages of grief.

Don't get me wrong, I was never angry with God for being led down the path I was on, but I did speak things out of my pain. There were a couple of times during my Red Devil chemo when I inquired of God on His whereabouts. I said, "Please, come down and let me feel you with me because I feel so alone." The truth is God was already with me; He never left me. But my pain caused me to not feel Him and to speak words I normally wouldn't have spoken, just like Job.

You all know how it feels when you're hurting. I don't know a single person who hasn't gone through some type of tragedy in life. Those who are reading this book have either been diagnosed with cancer, had someone in your family diagnosed, lost someone you love, suffered financial setbacks, or battled some type of trial or hardship. It's just life. Bad things happen to everyone, and we tend to want to know why. So we ask God—why?

When I first put it out on social media that I had breast cancer, I had support, for the most part. My friends rallied around with texts, calls, and messages telling me they loved me and were there for me. But, along with those who wanted to do good, also came those who wanted to do evil. I received messages from three people in particular who told me my cancer was a punishment for a past sin; one that had happened many years before, but one God had not forgotten about, and it was His way of "paying me back." I laughed when I read those messages because I know God isn't like that. He's a loving Father who doesn't wait for us to mess up so He can strike us with a horrible disease or a streak of misfortune in life. No, that's the way the world believes. They call it karma and think being guilty of a sin deserves suffering. That's not who God is at all. Yes, we do reap what we sow, but once we are forgiven and living in Christ and our sins have been covered by His blood and washed away, there is no more punishment for those sins.

So don't let anyone convince you that you have done something wrong and that's why you have cancer or any other illness in your body. There are a variety of things that cause cancer. Some are environmental, some are caused by the things we eat or drink, and some are just because; there is no answer, no rhyme nor reason. Not everything in life demands an answer. Sometimes, God uses things for His glory. So stop searching for *why* you have troubles, and start using those troubles to uplift God. Show the world that even in the midst of suffering, God is still good and still deserves to be praised.

The measure of spiritual maturity is not what happens to us over our lifetimes, but rather what we do *with* what happens to us. I used to hear the old-timers in church say, "Oh, I've been through a lot in life. If you haven't been through some hard trials, you need to question whether or not you're really saved."

I hated that. I didn't agree with judging my salvation against theirs based on how many battles I had fought in my life. I was younger than they were, by at least thirty years, and so it stood to reason I wasn't going to have faced all they had at that particular time in my life. That was the most ridiculous argument I had ever heard, to try to prove how religious they were. But that's another story for another time and place.

Again, I say, it's not the number of trials we go through, but rather the manner in which we endure them. It is never about how much strength we have in ourselves, but knowing

God's grace is sufficient in those times of trouble because His strength is made perfect in our weakness. 2 Corinthians 12:9 says, "Most gladly therefore will I rather glory in my infirmities, that the power of Christ may rest upon me."

Never look at your situation and boast in your own strength because I can tell you that outside of God, you have none. It takes His mercy and grace every day to even make it through what life has waiting for us when we wake up. And *never, ever* think just because you have a plan that your life will go accordingly. I am living proof that we can plan all we want but, in the end, it is up to God to choose the path on which we walk.

CANCER, GOD, AND ME

Eight

Cancer During a Pandemic... Oh Boy!!

"And the Lord said unto Him, Peace be unto thee; fear not; thou shalt not die."

- Judges 6:23

If you have lived on planet Earth during 2020 and 2021, you have clearly heard of Covid-19, the horrific virus whose only intention was to change life as we knew it by causing worldwide upheaval. The same can be said about cancer as well, except cancer (and everything else) took a back seat to this deadly virus for a year and a half.

From my understanding, we (America as whole) found out about Covid in January of 2020, but it wasn't until March that most of us actually became aware of it to the point that we realized it was going to be a real problem.

CANCER, GOD, AND ME

I can remember when I first found out it existed. I had begun seeing posts on social media, and it sounded frightening, so I started to research it for myself. I Googled it and read every article I found to figure out exactly what it was, how harmful it could be, and what I needed to do to protect myself and my son. I read that it was especially dangerous to those with compromised immune systems. Although I hadn't started taking chemotherapy yet, I was told cancer weakens the immunity somewhat, and I needed to be careful to not get Covid. Little did we know at that time that *everyone* needed to be careful regarding safety measures to prevent the virus.

On March 17, 2020, I had gone to the pharmacy to pick up my seizure medicine. I've had seizures since I was eighteen-months-old. They aren't bad, unless I get a fever, stay in the sun too long, or get the flu. So the medicine manages them and helps me to live a normal life. I was told to come back later because my prescription wasn't ready. I pulled my car into a parking spot and decided to make a video while I waited. I had already had my cancer blog page on Facebook that was titled, Cancer, God, and Me. Yes, just like this book. I made the decision when I was first diagnosed that I was going to document my journey so other women would be able to see what I would be going through and use it as a guide of what to do and what not to do. I wanted them to go with me as I was experienced every test, surgery, and emotion, so they would get their mammograms, do self-exams, and make sure to stay on top of their own health. I didn't want anyone to go through what was happening in my body and in my life.

By mid-March, I was making videos fairly regularly and uploading them to the page. I talked about my tests, the doctor's reports, and how I was feeling overall for any given day. Some of them were tear-filled, some had me reading Scripture, and some were just me pouring out all my feelings. I found it to be very cathartic. It felt as if I was only talking to myself as I spoke to my iPhone. I mean, no one was in my car, or my room when I did them, and so it was as if I was writing in a diary, except it was in video form. I honestly had no idea when I uploaded them they would end up helping so many women. I'm grateful they have because I wanted them to be of some use to someone, even if it was just one woman.

While I was making the video that day, it is evident I was struggling to breath. I was trying to talk about what was going on in general, but I was having trouble with my breathing. The virus didn't even cross my mind because it was still such a new illness, I didn't even think about it possibly being Covid-related. After a couple of hours, I really noticed my breathing getting worse. My arms were tingling, and I felt as if someone was hugging me so tightly they were cutting off my oxygen supply. I had Josh take my blood pressure, and it was extremely low. At 55/35, I knew something was terribly wrong. Josh suggested I let him take me to the emergency room, and I agreed.

When we got there, we were informed he could not go in with me because of the new precautions in place due to Covid. The doctor did an EKG, ran an arterial blood gas test to check my oxygen levels, and drew blood for labs. I was told in the interim I could possibly have a blood clot in my lungs or in my heart due to having had the lumpectomy. They then informed me I would probably need something called an angiography. They said that sometimes blood clots can happen after surgical procedures. But it had been a while since my procedure, and I wondered if that was even possible after a few weeks. But I didn't question them; they are the professionals, and who am I to argue?

In the meantime, I called a couple of elders from my church and told them what was going on. They immediately prayed for me and asked for Jesus to touch my body *right then*. While I was on the phone with them, I instantly started to breathe better. I began to feel the air flowing into my lungs with ease, and I knew I would be okay. Up until then, I was scared because I could not take in the amount of air I needed to function normally. I cannot explain how frightening that was.

There's something I want to say about the elders in my church and my church as a whole. They are the kindest, most humble people I have ever known in my life. I've been attending First Apostolic Church in Sevierville, TN for a little over three years, and I can't speak highly enough of them. The thing is, they want no praise or glory for themselves. When I say they are humble, I mean they embody the very definition of humility. They have given their entire lives and hearts to the Lord, and they live His Word every day. I strive to be like Pastor Carpenter, his wife, Sister Carpenter, Elder Erickson, and his wife, Sister Erickson. When you hear about how a Christian should live, these people are the examples of who Christ is on Earth. I am so blessed to have them in my life.

Once I started to feel better, Sister Erickson asked me to keep her updated on how I was doing, and then we hung up. The doctor came back in shortly thereafter and said they were going to do a chest x-ray before the angiography. I didn't understand what the angiography was or how it was performed, but it sounded scary, and I wanted no part of it. Was it a surgical procedure or a simple test? I had no idea.

CANCER, GOD, AND ME

Fast forward about two hours. I had been lying there, alone with only my phone. No visitors allowed made for a very sad day. I don't watch television, so when the nurse would pop in and offer to turn it on, I would just say no, thank you. There's only so much Facebook and Candy Crush you can take while lying in a hospital bed with IVs and the worry of some test you've never heard of.

The doctor finally came back in and told me that the x-ray showed I had bronchitis, and I would be given steroids and antibiotics and sent home. Praise God!! No angiography, no blood clots in my heart or lungs!! I cannot explain how relieved and happy I was the moment he said I didn't have blood clots. I called Sister Erickson to let her know the wonderful news that God had touched my body. I know it sounds odd for me to be happy that it was bronchitis but believe me when I say that something more than that *was* wrong when I first went it. As I look back, I wonder if I really did have Covid then and just didn't know it? After all, they didn't test me for it at the ER, so I will never know.

I do know, however, that because of the prayers of the elders from my church, God touched my body and let it be something minute in comparison to Covid. And that's what made me happy. I've had bronchitis in the past, and I'm not saying it's a walk in the park by any means, but I am so thankful it wasn't something worse, such as a blood clot or Covid-19.

Like everyone else in 2020, I spent most of the year in quarantine. Having cancer forced me to isolate, and Covid forced everyone else to isolate as well. While no one wants to have cancer, if it had to happen, I'm glad it happened during a pandemic. Most people say it was terrible that I was battling cancer during Covid-19 because no one could come see me, and they felt it made for a lonelier journey. I found it was easier for me knowing that others were wearing masks too. I didn't want to stand out as the only person wearing a mask when I did go out in public because then I was afraid people would look at me as if I was sick, and I didn't want that. I wanted to appear to be just like everyone else. So if everyone was wearing a mask, it meant I wouldn't stand out in the crowd, in a manner of speaking. So instead of looking at having cancer during Covid as a bad thing, I viewed it as the best time to have it. I know, my mind works in weird ways.

God has kept me safe during the pandemic. My son and

I wear masks everywhere we go, we use hand sanitizer, and we don't touch our faces. We wash our hands as soon as we get home, and we are careful to not pick up any more germs than we normally would overall.

We have been blessed throughout this journey to have had God's hedge of protection around us. In the book of Job, Satan told God the only reason Job loved God so much was because God had put a hedge around him and his household. Well, that is what a hedge of protection is. God will surround His children with His protection. Psalm 32:7 speaks of this very thing: "Thou art my hiding place; thou shalt preserve me from trouble; thou shalt compass me about with songs of deliverance. Selah." (KJV)

That is what His protection means for His children. God is my protector. Looking back, I can see He has been all of my life.

Nine

Time for Treatment, finally!

"I will instruct thee and teach thee in the way which thou shalt go: I will guide thee with mine eye."

-Psalm 32:8

Earlier, I said I always have a plan for everything. Well, I was chomping at the bit to finally get a treatment plan together and move forward through this mess of cancer. I've always been the type of person who sees the problem, identifies it, figures out a way to fix it, then plows into it, full steam ahead. I'm not sure if that's an asset or a liability. I feel for myself it's definitely a plus, but when I expect others to react to troubles the same way, it's a negative.

When asked to describe myself to anyone, I always say, "I'm a drill sergeant."

CANCER, GOD, AND ME

We've all seen the stereotypical military leaders portrayed on television as brash, tough, and strong. Well, that's how I've lived my whole life due to circumstances that produced those qualities in me.

Have I always been easy to live with or be friends with? I would say ask someone who is a friend, but I would have to say no, because I expect from others what I expect from myself, and that's not always fair. Some people cannot give you what they do not possess. I see people on social media who cry over things at which I wouldn't even blink an eye, and I want to say, "Get over it!" then I have to stop myself and remember we're not all alike, and the way I handle tough times might not be the way others do. I try to see where they are in their lives and what they've already been through or haven't been through.

The one who this has affected the most is my son. If you ask him how I raised him, he will probably say he felt like he was in the Army most of the time. That's not to say I never had compassion for him, but I taught him to never feel sorry for himself, and if he ever did have a pity party, to make it quick.

"Feel what you feel and get on with it!" I would say.

I know as humans, we must acknowledge our emotions, and we need to feel what we feel. But if we get stuck there, that sorrow can quickly turn into depression and that isn't a good place to live. So when I feel like I want to cry, I assess the situation first. Is it worth crying about? If not, then I shake it off and move on. If it is, then I allow myself to feel whatever emotion I have by letting the tears flow freely, then I get up and move on.

I make the conscious choice to not break down on Sorrow Avenue while on my way to Victory Lane! I feel everyone should live by that motto. Slow down, if you must, but keep that vehicle rolling. Perseverance, even in the face of death, will help you overcome many obstacles if you allow it.

I was glad to be going back to Dr. C's office to learn what we were going to do about this cancer in my breast and chest. Just knowing there was a plan of action being put into place gave me a spring in my step that I hadn't felt since before I was diagnosed.

It was March 19, 2020—two months since I had been given the horrible news. Covid had slowed everything down as far as doctor visits, surgeries, and tests. All elective procedures were being put off indefinitely, and only those surgeries considered emergencies were being done.

When I arrived at Dr. C's office, I didn't have a mask on because at that time the hoarders of the world had bought them all, and there were none to be found anywhere. My son spent almost an entire day going from super stores to drug stores to grocery stores looking for masks in our town and the neighboring county.

I pulled my cardigan up over my nose and went in. The nurse took me to the exam room, no questions asked. She didn't seem too concerned I wasn't wearing a mask, so I didn't think twice about it either. But when the doctor came in, he was upset about my being there. He asked why I had kept the appointment when I had symptoms of respiratory illness. I explained I had gone to the ER and was given a diagnosis of bronchitis. After a couple of minutes of him scolding me, he told me I would be meeting with the oncologist, Dr. O. on April 7th to get my plan of action.

Great! I thought.

My understanding was that Dr. C. would be the one who would have my "plan of action," but I guess I was wrong.

It seemed like we were playing a long drawn-out game of ping pong, and I was the ball. I was being bounced from this one to that one, here to there, and it felt as if I wasn't getting any answers. I knew the cancer treatment and surgeries were going to be a long process, but it had been over a month, and I still didn't have any definitive answers as to how things were going to play out over the next few months.

I just wanted the plan, for Pete's sake! I need a plan!

Incidentally, Dr. C. sent me to my primary care provider to get tested for Covid, and thank God the test came back negative a couple of days later.

Between the time of finding out when I would finally get my plan and actually getting to see the doctor who had it, I had my port put in. By getting that done, I felt like I was at least moving forward, however slowly, but I was moving, nonetheless.

Port placement surgery was going to be a breeze, or so I had been told by my fellow pink sisters in the online breast cancer support group to which I belonged. I had happened upon it one day on Facebook, and I joined, knowing I needed to be surrounded by women who were going through the same thing as I was. When you are given the news that you have anything wrong with you, you feel alone, and so it was important, vital even, that I found people who had experience and could help me navigate this new terrain.

Almost immediately I began asking questions, trying to prepare myself for whatever lay ahead.

"Is it going to hurt?" I asked, followed by, "How long will the surgery take? How long will it be sore? What does it feel like to have the port under your skin?"

There were so many things I wanted to know from those who had already been there, done that, and they were all there for me. I have found such a sisterhood in that group because we all share the same common bond—breast cancer, unfortunately. I want to say thank you to every woman in that group. I never could have gone through any of this without them. I have formed some wonderful friendships with women who truly love each other and have a desire to see each other not only survive but thrive.

March 24th was port placement surgery day. Again, I was a complete nervous wreck. You would think by that time I would've been very calm about being put to sleep. After all, that was to be my fourth surgery in ten months and fifth altogether. The year before I had to have a complete hysterectomy due to pre-cancer cells in my uterus, preceded by a hysteroscopy, and a few years before that, gall-bladder removal.

111 was my usual basket case self as my son drove me to the hospital that morning. As we waited for the nurses, anesthesiologist, and doctor to come in and do what they do pre-surgery, I could feel the anxiety stepping it up a notch. Although I tried to play it cool for his sake, Josh knew I was scared, and he offered to try to help with his usual dry humor and wit. Little did he know just his being there was all I needed to feel comforted.

Josh is my rock. I could not have beat cancer if it hadn't been for him. Having him there with me was enough to cause me to want to fight until I won if it meant giving me extra time with my son.

I never do well with anesthesia. I'm always so much groggier than what I should be and usually stay in recovery longer than they anticipate. And once back in my room, I'm still usually still drunk on the stuff past the point where I should be feeling normal. So any outpatient surgery I have, I always go home in a stupor. I've told my son with each surgery to NOT allow me to have access to my phone because I call people over and over and say things they cannot understand. And since I started my cancer blog, I make videos while still under the influence of anesthesia, which is hilarious looking back, but not when I post them to my page; that's horrifying. You should go over to the page and watch some of them if you need a good laugh, especially the one after my mastectomy.

Port placement was more difficult than what I had been told; or at least for me it was. The surgery itself wasn't too bad, except, like I said—the anesthesia. Afterward, my port stayed sore until it was removed in September.

It was nothing but trouble the entire time, but compared to getting chemo in my veins through a typical IV drip, it was the lesser of two evils. My veins are so tiny that lab technicians usually have a hard time drawing blood for regular lab work, let alone using them to push chemo every couple of weeks for six months. So, the port was the only option for me, really. I am glad I had it, don't get me wrong, but it hurt like the devil the entire time.

With the port installed, I was one step closer to finally getting the chemotherapy I so badly needed in order to get well. I was thankful to be where I was in the process, however long it seemed to be taking.

Ten

Well-Meaning Friends

"What are these wounds? Those which I got in the house of my friends."
-Zechariah 13:6

I said in a blog one day that cancer is the litmus test for a friendship. The dictionary describes it as a test that is used when one needs to find out the decisive factor for a situation. For example, when a politician is being reviewed for candidacy, he's asked a question to determine whether or not he should be moved forward in the process of nomination. If he gives the right answer, he passes the test; if not, then he won't be moved forward.

Well, when you have cancer and you tell people,

they're going to react one way or another. Either they will draw closer to you, or they will back away from you. I'm not here to bash anyone, but I do want you to know that if you find yourself in the place where you have to tell people you have cancer, don't be surprised when you lose a few friends.

You may ask, "Why would my friends leave me at such a horrible time in my life?" Well, it's not that complicated. Either they can take it, or they can't— bottom line. What I mean by that is not everyone can handle bad news. Not everyone is equipped to deal with what you've just heaped on them.

I can only speak for myself, but I'm going to tell you what happened to me. Again, please don't take this as me trying to hurt anyone who walked away from me. I'm only wanting to help other women to understand the whys of it all, when they begin to lose those they thought were the closest to them.

Not everyone runs away. Some people have tons of friends and extended family who rally around them and become one giant support group. I wasn't so fortunate to have that. I had moved here to East Tennessee on January 2, 2018. Being the outgoing, talkative people person I am, I made friends quickly. When I worked at Dollywood, I spoke to everyone in the park. That place employs almost four thousand people in the park alone, and it seemed as if I knew every one of them. A friend asked me one day how I had come to know so many people there in just a short few months. I told her I made it a point to speak to everyone, even if they didn't speak back. I find that people are friendly, and for the most part, they want to be spoken to and see a smile each day.

Don't get me wrong, there were some who were snobs, like the popular girls in high school who thought they were better than everyone, but I still said hello to them, smiled and let it go, even if they didn't greet me in return. But there were a few that I formed deep friendships with, or so I thought. There were two in particular to whom I had grown close. I have since learned that just because *I* feel close to someone doesn't necessarily mean *they* feel close to me. I guess I just took our friendship a little more seriously than they did.

In any event, both of those people let me down by walking away from me when I needed them the most.

Why?

Well, one of them was so wrapped up in her own stuff that she couldn't see past her life to realize that I honestly needed her.

And the other one? Well, I feel she truly couldn't handle my diagnosis. She is a very emotional, loving person who truly did care for me, but in that moment, she didn't know what to say or what to do. I feel she couldn't handle the thought of watching me suffer through chemo and be ill.

You see, there were two people who bailed on me for two different reasons. I wish they both would have just said, "Hey, we can't handle this; we're out of here," but they didn't. They left without a word, without a phone call, and without a care. And that was very difficult for me to process given the fact that I was already experiencing so much turmoil and sadness. I was so very hurt, and that is when I moved into the anger phase of the five stages of grief.

I realize my anger stemmed from my underlying issue of cancer, but it was easy to allow the anger to come out and be spewed onto those who hurt me, like the two friends. I was angry cancer had invaded my body, angry it had changed my plans, and angry it might take my life. I was angry that *I* had it when those who do nothing but live pure evil lives walk around cancer free! I was angry that those who had hurt me in the past now got to watch me suffer while they lived seemingly happy lives without any troubles at all. I was angry that those who hated me were now cheering for my death.

I was angry ... period. And those who hurt me were unfortunately going to feel the brunt of that anger.

We've all heard the saying, "You always hurt the ones you love."

Well, that's true, or at least it has been in my life. Like everyone else, I've made mistakes and bad choices which have led to the pain others felt, and ultimately caused me deep sorrow. In this case, my friend who seemed to ghost me was going to feel the sting of my pain. She had been telling me she was going to come visit me, and we could go for a drive. This was during the time when Covid was at its peak, and nothing was open, so driving around was all one could do. I would've enjoyed the sunshine and time with her. However, she never called me to set it up. So I decided I would call and ask her when she could come see me. That was mistake number one. I should *not* have called her. I should have simply let her do what she was capable of doing. But I honestly believed her when she said she wanted to come and visit me. I called, and she told me she wasn't available that day. After a few minutes of chatting, we hung up. Everything was fine. She texted me the next day and said she wanted to come get me and take me for a drive. Again, I believed her and waited for her. Waiting is all you have to do when you have cancer because you are out of work, and during the pandemic, you're not able to go anywhere. So my friend coming to take me for a drive was the equivalent of a child getting to go to a toy store. I was so looking forward to spending time with her. Once again, she didn't call or come, and once again like a fool, I called her and asked her what had happened. On that call she was different. She was rude and hateful, which was *not* in her character. She told me she was busy, and she couldn't come over at all. She hurt me. I felt like I had been lied to and led to believe something she never intended on doing at all. I felt like she had gotten my hopes up only to dash them. I was so wounded, I won't lie. So I texted her and told her that she lied to me and how much she had hurt me. I told her to forget my name and number because I wanted nothing else to do with her.

    Was that the right way to handle things? No, it wasn't. I immediately felt horrible for lashing out at my friend. But instead of apologizing like I knew I should, I used her actions toward me as a reason to try to justify my actions toward her. You've heard the saying, "Two wrongs don't make a right." Well, this was exactly what was happening. She was wrong, and I was wrong. Why did I lash out at her? The simple reason is because I was hurt, and to keep her from hurting me again, I wanted to hurt her to ensure she wouldn't call me and make empty promises anymore.

    I'm a college student working toward my master's degree in psychology and Christian counseling, so I know why we all do the things we do at times. But does that make me immune to acting in ways I know I shouldn't? No, it doesn't. First and foremost, I am a human being with feelings and emotions we all experience. And at that time, I was acting out of a place of anger, taking out my pain on my friend instead of the real enemy, which was the breast cancer. Cancer was an adversary I couldn't talk to or fight physically, but my friend was someone I could empty my frustrations onto and feel like I was justified. Walking away from her and the pain she was causing me allowed me to feel a sense of control I couldn't feel with the cancer. I couldn't tell it to leave me alone and then delete and block.

    I admit what I said to my friend in that text was wrong. Did I have the right to feel hurt by her actions? Absolutely. Our feelings are valid, and we must experience them. But we cannot let our feelings dictate our actions or we can get ourselves in a heap of trouble. We see it every day when people get upset at other drivers on the road and do things they should not. It's called road rage, and it can cost someone their life. Those are the ones who allow their emotions to dictate their behavior. I don't want to do that anymore. I hurt someone because she hurt me first. It was wrong ... period.

    I want to add that my friend and I have made up. I waited until I was better and out of treatment, and I called her and apologized to her for my part. She apologized for what she had done to me, and we let it go. It's too bad it had to happen in the first place, but it taught me a lot about people. And myself.

It taught me that some people just can't handle what you're going through, and that's okay. It's too painful for them to see their friend in pain. Now, is that selfish? Yes, in a way it is. They should put aside how they feel and concentrate on how the cancer patient feels. But as I said before, everyone isn't like me. Some people aren't as tough as nails, and they can't just plow through problems. Some people have to run away from them because of what they have gone through in life. My cancer was a painful reminder of what my friend had experienced with her own family member, and I didn't know that until we made up. If only we had discussed things in a civil manner instead of allowing emotions to rule our behaviors, things would've been a whole lot better. But hindsight is 20/20, and it's all over now. I'm thankful God allowed us to make up and be friends again. Our friendship will never be the same, but at least there was something to salvage.

Eleven

What is exactly is chemo?

"For I reckon the sufferings of this present time are not worthy to be compared with the glory which shall be revealed in us."
-Romans 8:18

Chemo is hard.

Let me rephrase that—chemo is the hardest thing I've ever gone through physically, and I never want to go through it again. There, that's better.

In April, I went to see the oncologist, Dr. O. He is one of the sweetest men I've ever met, and I'm forever grateful for his care of me. During that appointment, he told me the stage and grade of my cancer, how many treatments I would need, and the order in which I would receive each. It was to be four rounds of AC, twelve rounds of Taxol, the mastectomy, and then thirty-one radiation treatments. Wow! That was quite a plan. But a plan was what I wanted, right?

In case you've never heard of any of those before, let me try to break them all down for you. AC is short for the chemo cocktail made up of doxorubicin (Adriamycin) and cyclophosphamide. It is better known as the "Red Devil" around cancer centers and among those patients who have taken it. Why is it called the Red Devil? Because it is bright red—the color of the devil. It invokes thoughts of evil as soon as you look at it. I think the word chemo itself sounds evil, or at least it does to me. And I have heard—this is not fact, only rumor passed from one patient to another—that if spilled, AC can eat the linoleum off the floor in a matter of minutes. That was the stuff they were going to be putting into me! Okaaay!

Dr. O. explained to me the chemo would pass through the port that was now under my skin over my left breast. I tried not to think about that little purple piece of plastic inside of me because it gave me the willies!

How did I know it was purple? Because they had given me a pamphlet that I had to give to the nurse who would be administering the chemo so she would know the make and model of it and how to proceed accordingly. Make and model? Are we still talking about a small port or a car?

The very thought of having something foreign inside of my chest that was connected to my jugular vein was the most disturbing part of it for me. And when the doctor explained to me that the chemo would flow into the port, then pass through my heart before flowing out into my entire body, I was petrified. He spoke about it nonchalantly, as if he were explaining how a creek flows into the river. He spoke about it as if I knew as much about the subject as he did. But I didn't, and I was confused.

"What do you mean, the chemo will flow through my heart?" I was full of fear by that point. "Isn't that dangerous, though?" I asked.

Of course, it was dangerous. They were going to be pumping poison into my body for hours on end several times a month! But at that point in my journey, I honestly didn't know how bad it was. Don't get me wrong, I had heard about people being sick from chemo, but I had never been around anyone who had it, so I didn't know what it entailed. All I knew was that the very word "chemo" instilled a fear in me that was only beaten out by the word "cancer."

The doctor looked at me as I spouted my ridiculous but genuine questions. I saw confusion in his eyes. He knew it was dangerous, and I think he may have been caught off guard by my questions. He seemed to not know what to say.

"Well, having breast cancer is more dangerous than the treatment itself. Yes, you will get sick," he said as he got his pen and paper. "Let me show you by drawing it."

I watched as he drew what appeared to be a line of about four to five images of the letter U. He explained that the chemo would cause my white blood count to drop dramatically.

"You're currently here at the top of this U," he said as he pointed. "But the chemo will cause your immune system to drop down to here." He pointed at the bottom of the first U. "But during your week off, your body will somewhat heal itself so you will come up a little in time for your next dose of chemo. Does that make sense?" He asked as he placed the pen on the table.

I remember just staring at the paper. He had just drawn it and explained it in such a sterile manner, as if he were a robot. I'm sure it's because he does it many times a day, and by that point in his career it had become routine for him. It would be the same way I explained the alphabet to my son when he was a toddler. I knew what the letters were, but my son didn't, and he had to learn. Dr. O. knew what he was talking about, but it was complete Greek to me.

"So in the week I'm not having chemo, I'll get better?" I asked, still so new to it all.

"Well, you won't get better, as you say," he replied. "But you will start to feel somewhat better. Enough to be able to tolerate the next round. Normally, we only give this chemo every three weeks, but since you have Triple Negative, we have to give it every other week."

His voice seemed to have a faint echo. Every word he spoke sounded as if it was repeating itself in a lower tone. They went into my ears and got lost somewhere in my brain. My heart raced faster with each thing he told me. I felt lightheaded and sick to my stomach.

God, please don't let me puke on this man's shoes!! I thought as I sat there staring at him. He had the prettiest, softest blue eyes I have ever seen. And even though his mask covered most of his face and mouth, somehow the appalling words, chemo and triple negative, seemed to pierce through just fine.

He sat there, silent. I'm sure the look on my face must have matched what was going on in my mind, and he was giving me the time and space needed to process what had just been said.

"Why can't I wait the usual three weeks?" I asked him when I could finally bring myself to speak. I was wanting to put it off for as long as I could.

He explained that Triple Negative is the worst type of breast cancer a woman can have. It is the most aggressive and most deadly type, and doctors have to attack it hard and fast. He told me it wasn't good that I was already in the stage and grade I was, so waiting any longer would be detrimental to me.

I realized at that point I had no choice but to go headfirst into it without reservations and fear. This was going to be something I couldn't do on my own.

The room was quiet. The doctor, the NP, and a lady who was called the Nurse Navigator were in there with me, and no one was speaking. Were they giving me time to get my thoughts in order?

"I feel like you're speaking to someone else," I finally said as I broke the deafening silence.

I looked behind me and then back to the doctor. "It's as if there is someone else in here with us, and you're talking to them and not me. There is no way this is my life!" I said with tear-filled eyes.

I shook my head, and the tears dropped to my legs. The nurse practitioner handed me a tissue, and they all just looked at me. It was so sterile. Don't get me wrong, they are very kind people, but no one was hugging me, no one was telling me I was going to be okay. Instead, the doctor was giving me my itinerary for the next six months, and the others were taking notes.

I wanted to get up and leave. I wanted to run away as fast as I could. I wanted to be anywhere but there! But I couldn't. I was told if I didn't get treatment I would most likely die by the end of the year. That was *not* an option for me, and it was all I needed to hear to snap back to reality and get it started. Triple Negative breast cancer is no joke. Let me rephrase that—*cancer is no joke*, but the kind I had was like the Terminator of cancers. It was strong, aggressive, mean, and cruel. It had come for my life, but what it didn't know was that it had picked the wrong woman to mess with!

I wiped my eyes and listened intently to every word he said. I followed along as he told me what to expect and how I would feel. I watched as he wrote down dates and numbers, and I felt a fire rise up inside of me. I knew neither cancer nor the Red Devil would extinguish. I was ready to fight. Cancer started it, but I was going to finish it with the help of God!

Bring it on, chemo!

CANCER, GOD, AND ME

Twelve

Here We Go… Buckle Up

"Many are the afflictions of the righteous: but the Lord delivereth him out of them all."
-Psalm 34:19

Before chemo even begins, every patient must undergo a couple of tests to be sure their health is good enough to withstand the poison about to be deposited into their already dying bodies. That kind of sounds like an oxymoron, doesn't it? It reminds me of a boxer who trains to get in shape to climb into the ring and get beat up. Sounds like a waste of time, but what do I know?

An echocardiogram, or ultrasound of the heart, is one of those tests. It is done to ensure the heart is strong enough to withstand what chemo is about to do to it. Trust me when

CANCER, GOD, AND ME

I tell you *chemo hurts every part of your being*. From your blood, tissues, muscles, skin, to your organs, chemo can be a silent killer. I won't bore you or scare you with all the details of what it does to each part of the body; you can research it if you like. I will tell you chemo is dangerous, more dangerous than we really understand when we are first faced with having to get it. I always tell my son if I knew then what I know now, I'm not sure I would've gone through it. If ever faced with recurrence of breast cancer (which is a real possibility with triple negative) I doubt that I will fight it again; chemo is that hard.

In 2010, my primary care doctor discovered that I have three leaky heart valves. I was getting a routine physical, and my blood pressure happened to be extremely low that day. It caused him concern, and he referred me to a cardiologist. I was instructed by the doctor to walk every day to strengthen my heart. After all, the heart is a muscle, and muscles benefit from exercise.

During my echo, a few days before chemo, I was watching the screen to see what my heart was doing. I had become accustomed to what I was seeing during the test. From 2010 to 2020 I had, had several echocardiograms to make sure the leaky valves hadn't gotten worse. I knew what the blue and red colors meant and how it all flowed, or was supposed to flow, and I recognized the valves and the speed at which they lifted and closed or didn't close all the way, which was what mine had always done. That was what denoted they were leaky. I'll spare you the drawn-out medical lesson. Feel free to research it yourself.

At any rate, before every test I have, before every surgical procedure, and before every single doctor's appointment, I always text or call Elder Erickson and ask for prayer. The Bible says in James, "Are there any sick among you? Let him call for the elders of the church; and let them pray over him, anointing him with oil in the name of the Lord: and the prayer of faith shall save the sick; and the Lord shall raise him up." (5:14-15) I know enough about God to know He absolutely hears us when we cry out to Him, and He does move on our behalf. I trust He hears me every single time I pray, and He is willing to help me in my time of trouble. God wants us to trust Him completely. He wants us to know and have faith that He will never leave us. Hebrews 11:6 says, "But without faith it is impossible to please Him; for he that cometh to God must believe that He is, and He is a rewarder of them that diligently seek Him." If you have any knowledge of the Bible whatsoever, then you know that every person who was healed by Jesus first had faith that He *could* heal them. That is why they came to Him in the first place, because they believed.

I've always known of the healing power of Jesus, and I have never doubted it or been ashamed of the gospel of Christ. So when it came time to go on the cancer journey, I felt assured I would have Jesus right by me. As David said in Psalm 23, "Yea, though I walk through the valley of the shadow of death, I will fear no evil, for thou art with me." I knew the Lord was with me, and I could call on Him, and my brothers and sisters at church could call on Him whenever I needed Him. I am like a child in that way. I have always believed people and what they say. If you tell me that you will call me at two in the afternoon, I will believe you. If you don't call, then I am more likely not to believe you the next time you say it. I believed God when I first heard of His promises, and He never let me down; He always came through for me. So, it stood to reason I would believe Him during my cancer journey. He hadn't let me down yet, and I knew He never would. I believe every word in the Bible. I can stand firm on the promises of God.

Before the echo, I called on Sister Erickson and her husband to pray for me. They did, and I went on. During the test, I watched the screen. When I got my results, the oncologist nurse practitioner told me I didn't have any leaky heart valves and my heart was normal. I wasn't sure I'd heard her correctly, and I asked her to repeat what she had just told me. She said my echo showed everything was normal. But how? I'd had leaky heart valves since 2010; I'd been told by two different cardiologists I had three of them. I was so happy my heart had now returned to normal, and I knew exactly who had healed it—*Jesus*!

Of course, I called the elders after my appointment and told them how everything showed all clear and how I didn't have the problem anymore. They were happy for me as well, and we gave God the glory for it all. Sister and brother Erickson are the humblest people I know, and they always make sure that instead of giving them praise that I give God all the glory. I understand where they are coming from because I do the same thing when others say I am the strongest person they know; I make sure to tell them it is God who gives me the strength they see and not myself. I am nothing without Him.

So with the echo having wonderful results, the port in place, and having my plan of action, all that was left was to begin chemotherapy. The nurse practitioner asked me if I was ready, and I forced a smile and told her yes. But I wasn't. I was petrified at the thought of having poison distributed into my body in just a few short minutes from then. Before I stood up, I asked her if I would die. I know it sounds silly, but my biggest fear was that as soon as the nurse connected the bag of meds, I would just die. I had a couple of friends who had been telling me a few weeks before that their family members had experienced an overdose and one of them even died because of chemo.

Wow! Really? You're going to tell that to someone who has cancer and is getting ready to begin chemo? Tell me how you think that is helpful at all? I'll wait...

Right, it's not!

I never said anything to them, but I could've gone the rest of my life without hearing that and been better for it. Before I go any further, I want to say, if you have never had cancer, and if you happen to be a friend, family member, or you're a caregiver of someone who is battling this horrific disease, *do not* add to what they're already going through by telling them horror stories of people who've had bad experiences with chemo or radiation. Don't be a negative person and bring fear into their lives. Cancer patients are already fighting distress, sorrow, anger, and the disease itself without someone else adding in their two cents about how dangerous treatment can be.

I'm sorry to sound harsh but I know from first-hand experience that having others tell you negative things when you're looking for positive stuff to focus on is not the way to help.

Remember the old saying, "If you don't have anything nice to say, then say nothing at all?" Well, when someone has cancer, you really should practice that before you open your big mouth!

When my friends told me about those two people, it really was the moment that fear struck my heart and mind, and it took a lot of sleepless nights in prayer for God to lift that fear from me. I didn't want to die from the one thing that could possibly save my life.

The nurse practitioner calmed my fears by telling me that chemo wasn't going to kill me, and the nurses would keep an eye on me the entire time I was there. She said one of them would even sit with me if needed to calm me down. That made me feel a whole lot better about what I was getting ready to go through.

She showed me to the infusion room where I saw eight recliners in a semi-circle around the room; each separated by a large heavy curtain. The wall behind them was all windows, and the sun was shining through. I was taken to a chair, where I sat and tried to get comfortable. I turned on my phone camera and began to record a bit of my first chemo session. My legs and hands were shaking terribly. I explained to the nurse that I kept a vlog and how I posted it to my social media page. I promised her I would not show her face, the face of any medical personnel, or of the patients to protect the privacy of everyone there. She nodded and then proceeded to tell me in detail what she was doing.

She explained the process of how she was giving me pre-meds, which consisted of two anti-nausea medicines, and how she was also going to give me a steroid that would counteract any allergic reaction I might have to the chemo itself. I could feel my heart beating faster with each word she spoke, and I started to sweat. I was petrified! I closed my eyes and prayed silently for God to be there with me as I tried to soothe myself by taking slow breaths in through my nose and slowly exhaling out of my mouth. I found that breathing technique to be the best for me in any situation where I was stressed, scared, or angry. It allows your mind to focus on something besides what's happening to you in that moment.

It took the pre-meds about an hour to slowly go into my system. Now, it was time for the chemo itself. I'm not going to lie and pretend to be some tough woman who stood face-to-face with this process without any fear. No, I was a total basket case by the time she brought those two big syringes to me. She laid them on the small table in front of my recliner, scanned my bracelet and then the medicine tubes. That was something they did with every single tube or bag, every single time they administered a different medicine. Talk about being careful. Knowing they had all of those precautions in place gave me an added sense of security. I could check one thing off my list of worries. But, come on, they're professionals who hold lives in their hands; of course they're going to be attentive to every aspect of the process.

Her hands seemed to move in slow motion as she picked up the first vile and connected it to the line going into my port. I turned my head to the other side because I couldn't watch. I didn't want to see the Red Devil as it now became a part of me and flowed throughout my body. I tried to tell myself it was for my good and it was my friend. I tried to convince myself chemo wasn't going to hurt me but help to heal me.

She sat next to me, slowly pushing the syringe as it emptied of the red liquid. She disconnected it and hooked up the next one. She asked me every couple of minutes how I was feeling, and I told her that I was fine other than feeling like I might die at any moment.

Once she was done, she took my blood pressure and said that it was good. I told her that I couldn't feel the chemo in me at all. She reassured me again I wouldn't be able to feel it, but the side effects would begin that night or the next day. At first, I would feel energetic because of the steroids, then I would crash because of the chemo. I dreaded it.

Nothing she said to me that day could've prepared me for what the chemo really did to me. It was horrible. If I tried right now to explain to you in detail what happened in my body and how I felt, you still couldn't grasp just how bad it all was. It's something you have to experience yourself to truly understand, but something I pray no one has to go through. I pray every day for a cure for this grisly disease.

It's estimated that roughly 906 new cases of breast cancer will be diagnosed *every day* in 2021. Those include both invasive and non-invasive (in-situ) for a total of 330, 840 cases this year alone. And of those, about 43,000 women are expected to die from breast cancer this year. This is heartbreaking to me. With all the money spent on research to find a cure, the rate of death has only declined 1% per year between 2013 and 2018, for a total of 6% (breastcancer.org)[3]. While that is 6% and we can look at that as a positive, I still wish breast cancer and all types of cancer could be eradicated.

After approximately four hours, I was finished having my body filled with toxins. Although I didn't feel any different physically, in my mind, I felt like I was now in some kind of science experiment where they had taken the best of me and mix it with the worst of something else to create some kind of monster. I almost expected to be able to leap onto a building or stop a train by that point; boy, was I wrong.

I left the cancer center filled with mixed emotions. While I was happy to finally be in active treatment because it meant I would be able to begin the arduous process of healing, I hoped. Even though I was now being given the strongest medicine I could get to kill the cancer, I still had no idea if it would work or if I would survive. After all, women died every day of breast cancer; just read the statistics. But at least I was on my way to healing with some type of treatment plan now underway.

Once I got home, I wanted to eat ... everything! Those steroids were causing me to want things I hadn't had in a long time, and so I had pizza, along with some fruit and instant mashed potatoes and peas.

That night, after I had calmed down and found some peace in my heart and mind, I went into my bathroom. When I saw all of my brushes, hair bands, bobby pins, and shampoos sitting there, I broke down. The thought of losing my hair was causing me more pain than I realized it would.

I want to state emphatically—if you have NOT had cancer and lost your hair or your breasts—DO NOT ever tell a cancer patient, "It's only hair; it will grow back," or

"They're only boobs; you don't need them." That is the most hurtful things you could ever say to someone who is facing something you know nothing about! If I seem angry in my writing, it's because I am. I had several people say those exact words to me, and it hurt. Actually, it made me angry! When spoken to me, I immediately countered with, "You've never been through this, so you don't get an opinion or get to tell me how to feel!"

I will say that I realized their reasons for saying what they did; they were only trying to help, but they were going about it in the absolute worst way, the wrong way. I'll give you an example: If I have never jumped out of an airplane, then how can I expect to comfort someone who is standing at an open door of a plane with their parachute, getting ready to fling themselves out and hurtle toward the ground at a high rate of speed? I can't.

And neither can anyone who has never experienced cancer. You can't give advice on what you haven't experienced. I needed to drop that in here. If you're a patient who is reading this, and you're going through something similar, bookmark this page and lend it to the one who is saying hurtful things. If you can't bring yourself to tell them how you feel, my words might enlighten them.

Now back to the bathroom and all my hair things in

front of me. I knew the loss of my hair was approaching more quickly now that I'd had the chemo in my body. It was my understanding it would take anywhere between ten–fourteen days for me to begin seeing it either in the shower or on the pillowcase. My heart ached at the prospect of finding my hair on the floor or on my clothes. I was afraid to imagine what I would look like with a bald head. Was my head shaped pretty? Was it pointy and knobby? Were my ears so big that I would look like Dumbo without hair to cover them? Those were all valid questions that were ripping through the gray matter of my brain, and I was tired of thinking about it. I wanted it to go away.

In case you haven't realized it by now, I'm a person who wants things to just go away, but life doesn't work that way. When we find ourselves on the battlefield, we ***must*** fight. There is no giving up or wishing that our enemy will just go away. So I had to face the fact that I was going to be bald very soon and for a good while. But what could I do about it? Nothing. It was imminent, and it was coming rapidly.

I began putting away things I knew I wouldn't need for at least the next year, such as my hair dryer, brushes, hair masks, ponytail bands, etc. I put them in a basket and hid them under the sink. Out of sight, out of mind, right? Not quite. It would still hurt me every day thereafter for months. I would terribly miss not being able to put my long blonde hair up in a messy bun on top of my head and throw on my sunglasses. I would miss standing in front of the mirror while blowing it dry and then curling it just right. I would miss twirling it around my finger when I was tired (a habit I'd picked up when I was little). But there was nothing I could do to change any of it.

That night, I went to bed with the steroids still pulsing through my veins. My heart rate was racing, and my legs felt as if they were running under the blanket. Try as hard as I could, they would not stay still, and it was so frustrating. I would later come to find out that restless leg syndrome is a side effect from the steroids. When I say restless leg, I mean, restless! It was awful. I wanted to sleep so badly, but my legs seemed to want to dance. My foot was tapping furiously on my mattress, and I couldn't control it.

Is this what it's going to be like for the next few months? I thought as I laid there stiff as a board, thinking that would somehow help. It didn't.

My body finally gave in to exhaustion. I fell asleep and woke up early the next morning. That day wasn't too bad. I remember only feeling slightly sick, as if I were getting a cold. I felt rundown a tad. *This isn't too bad,* I said to myself as I tried to clean house. I quickly realized that my normal strength was gone, and I sat down. How was it that chemo was hitting me already? I mean, I had only gotten it the day before. Shouldn't it have given me some time to get used to the idea of having it in my body before it assaulted me like that? How rude!

Two days post treatment, the chemo effects were in full swing. I woke up to a headache, sore throat, nausea, and intense shaking. My son asked if I was okay, and all I could do was ask him to look up the side effects of Red Devil and see if shakiness was one of them. After a minute or so, he informed me that it was normal.

Great!! I thought. Along with everything else, now I was going to shake like a leaf on a tree in a windstorm. But I didn't have a choice. I was going to have to buckle down and know that no matter what came my way as far as illness, I would ride it out with the Lord by my side. He was the one I could always count on to never leave me, and I was about to need Him more than I ever had before.

When a patient has chemo, he or she goes for the actual

infusion one week and then for a checkup the next week to see how they're doing. Oncologists monitor the patient very closely. I've never been watched so carefully in my life, and I cannot thank my doctors enough for the level of care they provided me. My first checkup after chemo was the following Tuesday, exactly one week later. I was taken into the infusion room, had my blood drawn through my port, then taken to an exam room where I would wait for the nurse practitioner. When she came in, I was informed that I had lost four pounds that week, something they didn't want me doing. I lost a total of thirty pounds over the next five months (all of which I have put back on to date). She also let me know that my white blood count was extremely low, but that was to be expected every single week. I told her I was weak, and my legs felt exhausted (also something that continued and only got worse due to my hemoglobin being dangerously low). I was also dehydrated and anemic. She gave me sample bottles of Ensure and Boost and told me if I wasn't able to eat, then I needed to, at the very least, drink those and have my son get more at the store. She explained that maintaining my weight up and keeping my strength were paramount to staying strong during chemo treatment. Over the following weeks, I would have to occasionally go to the cancer center and have IV fluids to help counteract the dehydration that happened without fail.

April 28th, two weeks after my first infusion, I was scheduled for my second. I dreaded it just as much as the first. I had just begun to feel better on Sunday, and here it was time for another treatment to put me back down. I went through the usual routine of labs, infusion, etc. and I went home. The next few days were carbon copies of those the previous two weeks, except for one difference. Two days after my second dose, the thing I had been dreading happened; my hair started to fall out. I woke up one morning and rolled over to find a large piece of my long blond hair had managed to come out overnight and was resting on my bed next to my pillow. I knew in that moment it was time to say goodbye to a piece of me. I cannot explain the pain in my heart that I experienced when I saw it. I cannot expect you to understand how deeply it hurt unless you've gone through it too. If you haven't, then please know it is the equivalent of losing a friend. You see, we've had our hair ALL of our lives. We've never seen ourselves bald before, or most of us haven't. We love our hair, and we care for it daily. We get it cut, shaped, and colored. We put treatments on it and style it in pretty ways that make us look more attractive. The Bible even says our hair is our glory and is given to us for a covering, so it must be pretty important. (1

Corinthians 11:5). At any rate, my hair meant more to me than what I had even realized.

I didn't cut it that day, although I had been advised to do so by my pink sisters in the support group. By the way, the term pink sisters refer to those women who are bonded by breast cancer. Although we aren't related by blood, we are sisters by way of the common bond of breast cancer. I had been told that as soon as my hair started to come out, the best thing to do would be to shave my head. I couldn't do it. As many times as I'd thought about it, I couldn't bring myself to pick up my son's clippers and shave it all off. It was simply too painful to imagine.

It was time for my next checkup, and I decided to hide the huge bald spot on the right side of my head, I would wear a ball cap. No one would even notice, and I could go on "pretending" everything was okay. For my blog page, I took a picture of myself in the waiting room of the cancer center. Before I uploaded it, I looked at how thin my hair had become, and I realized I was only delaying the inevitable. After a little thought and a lot of prayers for strength, I made up my mind to shave it off and get it over with.

When I got home, I asked my son to bring his clippers to me and leave me alone for a while. I reached for my scissors, took a deep breath, and made the first cut. My hair was well below my shoulders, so cutting it up to my ear was devastating. But once I made the first cut, I was at the point of no return. I continued to cut it all around my head as best as I could until it was almost all gone. All that remained was some sort of funky, weird bits of hair that belonged in a horror movie. I was in too deep to stop at that point. It didn't even have a style; it was just chopped into a million oddball pieces that were sticking out and up. I plugged in the clippers and began to shave my head. Less than a minute in, I had to stop. I couldn't do it. Cutting my hair was one thing, but there was no way I could bring myself to take those clippers over my head and rid myself of the last bits of my beautiful hair.

I sat down and cried. "How did I get here?" I asked myself aloud as I looked in the mirror. "How did I end up with cancer?" I shouted a little louder.

Yep, I was still in the anger phase of grief.

I dried my eyes and went to ask my son if he could finish the job for me. Don't misunderstand me, asking my son to shave my head wasn't something I wanted him to do. He was my son, and I didn't want that to become a memory for him for the rest of his life. He had offered earlier in the week, and I had turned him down. He reassured me that if it came to it, then he was willing. Well, it came to it.

He agreed with a smile on his face. Of course, he wasn't happy about it, but I think it made him feel like he was a part of what was going on. I believe it was a way for him to take some sort of control in the whole cancer journey as well; or at least feel as if he had.

He shaved my head as I cried. He kept telling me what a nicely shaped head I had, how it was going to look amazing, and how I was going to rock a shaved head. I appreciated his encouragement, but I knew otherwise. I wasn't going to rock a bald head. I wasn't going to look amazing. I was going to look like a woman who had cancer, and that was the last thing I wanted.

Wait, was this truly about my hair or the fact that I would finally have to face the fact that I was sick?

I mean, up until that point, I looked healthy. I even had someone tell me, "You don't look sick," which I loved! I didn't want to look sick. I didn't want to look like a cancer patient. I wanted to go through this looking as normal as possible. There were days when I would go to my appointments and see the other patients and ask myself how I ended up there with them. I couldn't wrap my head around the fact that I was one of them; that I had cancer. I tried to not think about it.

Looking back now, I can see I had compartmentalized

it. I was putting it somewhere else and concentrating on other things—school, my son, anything. I had thrown myself into my studies, and finals were coming up. Who had time to worry about cancer? Even my doctor told me at my chemo appointment that week I was incredibly upbeat and positive, and she explained how patients who kept that attitude were the ones who usually had a greater chance of survival.

Well, that's all I needed to hear to ensure I would stay alive. In other words, if *I* could improve my chances of living just by being happy and upbeat, then happy and upbeat it was going to be. I was going to put cancer out of my mind (as much as possible) and go on about my business of school and life with my son.

When Josh was done, I looked at myself in the mirror. Who was that woman staring at me? I didn't recognize her at all. There were no more long blonde locks, but instead a head covered in a dark buzz cut. I looked as if I was scheduled to be at boot camp the following day. I hated it. But there was nothing I could do. This was my journey, like it or not.

Josh hugged me. "It's okay, Mom. You still look pretty," he said with a compassion in his voice that only comes from pure love. When I tell you my son is an amazing human, I mean it. He is the kindest, most decent, most loving person

I have ever known. Am I biased? Maybe, but if you have the pleasure of knowing him, then you will say the same things I say about him. He truly is a blessing from God.

I mustered a smile, just for him. "Thank you," I said and went to my bed and laid down.

He unplugged the clippers and walked out of my room. The tears began to flow heavily after he was gone. I was alone, and it was okay to cry. I prayed to God to help me accept the fact that for the next few months I wasn't going to have any hair at all.

About half an hour later, my son walked into my bedroom and his shiny bald head announced itself.

"What have you done?" I asked him as I sat up in shock.

He smiled. "I shaved my head in honor of you."

At that moment, my heart could've burst with love and pride in my son. But my eyes burst instead. I began to cry, and I grabbed him and hugged him so tightly. It's one thing to know someone will be by your side at the hardest time in your life, but to see them shave their head for you is entirely a different thing. It drove home his commitment to me, his mother. After that day, I never doubted his willingness to do anything to help me get well.

I won't bore you with the details of every doctor's appointment and chemo treatment after that. But I will say there were things going on in my body I had never experienced before. I stayed dehydrated and had to go to the local ER every other week after chemo. I began having multiple grand mal seizures a day, another side effect from chemo and dehydration, and my doctor increased my dosage of Keppra. I was so weak I couldn't walk, and my son had to lead me to the bathroom. I went from spending three days in bed at the beginning of chemo to spending six days in bed. I wasn't doing well at all. I was going to need God to touch my body, and I was willing to pray all night to get it.

CANCER, GOD, AND ME

Thirteen

The Day Jesus Healed Me!

"And he said unto her, Daughter, thy faith hath made thee whole; go in peace and be whole of thy plague."
-Mark 5:34

This is probably my favorite chapter in my cancer ordeal because I not only get to recall the way the Lord healed me, but I also get to tell others all about His goodness. And that's something I love to do every chance I get. I'm known for saying, "I wish I had a microphone and a giant mountain I could stand on and just tell everyone about how good God is." Well, this book might just be my microphone and my mountain on which I'm able to tell everyone about Him. He is a wonderful counselor, the mighty God, the Prince of Peace, my comforter, healer, best friend, and the love of my life. He's there when no one else is. He never leaves me alone. Even when I didn't want Him, He still held on to me. That is a love that you and I will never know in this world.

Let me tell you how it came about on the day He touched my body. It was Sunday, June 7th, 2020, a day I will never forget. A day I won't stop talking about to everyone who will listen.

I was on my "off week" from chemo and scheduled to go back for the next dose on Tuesday. I had just finished with the Red Devil the week before, and it had definitely delivered its cumulative punch, just as I had been told it would. By this time, I was so weak and frail I wasn't even able to walk around my own bedroom without my son literally wrapping his arms around me and propping me up. He would help me out of the bed and hold my arm as I took the few steps into my bathroom and then make my way back to bed. I wasn't getting up at all except to go to the bathroom. My son was doing all of the cooking, laundry, housework, shopping, along with working full time (from home because of Covid) and taking college classes.

I'm sure he was overwhelmed with everything, but he never let it show. He never lost his temper or complained at all. He was phenomenal, and I knew God had given him a strength that could only come from Him. I had always known my son loved me, I'm his mom and of course he did, but during this time in my life, I knew without a doubt he would always be there to take care of me if I needed him. He's going to make an amazing husband one day.

In the days leading up to Sunday, I had an immense urge to go to church. It was as if I knew I needed to be there on that particular day at that particular service. I can't explain how I felt the drawing, but if you've ever experienced it before, then you know, and you understand that when God is bidding you to do something, you need to obey.

I mentioned to my son that I wanted to go, and he asked if I was able to actually get up to even get myself ready. I told him I knew God was bidding me to be there, and I had to listen to Him, no matter how long it would take me to get ready. He agreed to drive me, and I patiently waited for Sunday to come.

The Sunday service at my church starts at 2:00 in the afternoon because we have two campuses, and our pastor goes to one and then comes to ours and then back to the other one at night. I love that we don't have to get up so early and go, and it sure did come in handy that day. I woke up early and began my daunting task of trying to raise up and take all of my morning medicines. When I was finished, my son helped me into the bathroom where I was barely able to take a quick shower before feeling like I would pass out. I sat on the edge of the tub and dried my body as I tried to regain any strength I could. My son got my skirt and blouse and helped me to get dressed. I had to sit on my bed with a makeup mirror because I wasn't able to stand up for any amount of time. I slowly began drawing on my eyebrows and putting on eyeliner in an attempt to not look like a corpse. Chemo had taken every hair from my body, including my lashes and brows, so anything I could do to add a little color here and there made me feel like I didn't look as scary as I really did. There was something about being sick that I honestly didn't notice *when* I was sick. I guess it was because I either didn't pay much attention to myself or maybe it was where I saw myself every day and had grown accustomed to seeing that person in the mirror. Looking back at pictures from last summer, I see just how ill I was.

I finished with what makeup I felt like applying and put on my shoes. I texted my friend to see if the church had a wheelchair I could use to get inside, and she told me one would be waiting for me at the door. My spirit was excited, but I couldn't get my body to come up to the same level. All it wanted to do was go back to bed, but my soul thirsted for

God's presence that we can only feel in church sometimes. The Bible speaks in Hebrews 10:25 of not forsaking to assemble ourselves together. Fellowship with other believers is one of the most important aspects of our walk with God. Although, when you're sick and can't get to church, God completely understands, and there is no shame or condemnation in that. But when you are well, it's a good thing to go to the house of God.

The excitement that filled my heart and the joy I felt when my son pulled into the parking lot are indescribable. It had been a long time since I had gone to church because of treatments and also because of the fact the church had been closed for a couple of months due to Covid. But now, they were open once again, and I was ready to be with my brothers and sisters in Christ.

My son parked the car in one of the available spaces and went inside to get the wheelchair. I could feel the presence of God right there in my car already beginning to stir something inside of me. I knew without a doubt I was exactly where I was supposed to be that day. My son helped me slowly move from the car to the chair, and then he pushed me into the building. Our temperatures were taken, we were offered hand sanitizer, instructed not to hug anyone, or shake hands, and to stay six feet apart. That wasn't going to be a problem for me since I had been living that way for months due to my white blood cell count sitting at nearly zero every week at my checkups.

We were shown to an open spot in the back that was large enough for the wheelchair to sit in without being in the way of others coming in. My heart was happier than it had been in months, and I settled in for what I knew was going to be an extraordinary service. Everyone was waving at me, saying they had missed me, and had been praying for me. I was waving back and wishing I could see their smiles, but masks sadly prevented that from happening. Oh well, I was at church, and I was going to make the most of it, even masked up and socially distanced, because I had no idea when I'd get to go again.

The choir began to sing, and I thought my heart would burst with happiness and love. I realized at that very moment what David meant when he said in Psalm 122, "I was glad when they said unto me, let us go into the house of the Lord." That has always been one of my favorite passages of Scripture and right then I finally realized its true meaning. Though I have to admit my heart had started rejoicing days earlier when I made the decision to go to church. I had a mission—get to the church, where Jesus was.

The night before, on Saturday, God brought to my

remembrance a passage in the Bible where some men took their sick friend to the house where Jesus was one day, and when they could not get the man in the door because of the crowd, they cut a hole in the roof and let him down to Jesus (Luke 5). That is faith!! They had all heard of the miracles Jesus was performing, and they believed if they could just get their friend to where He was, Jesus would heal him. And heal him, he did! The Bible says when Jesus saw their faith, He healed the man and forgave his sins.

What is the one word that comes up over and over again in the Bible regarding healing?

F A I T H.

Five letters that make all the difference in the world. Five letters that determine whether or not you're healed. I believed God had bid me to come to church that day as a test of my faith in order to heal me. Now, I could have said, "God, I'm just too weak to go," and I would've been justified in that because I was indeed very ill. I could've said, "I can't get ready and make the trip," and it would've made sense because it was one of the hardest things I have done, to get ready that day in the shape I was in physically. But I did it anyway. Not to boast in myself, but I boast in the Lord. He gave me the strength it took to get ready. I believe when He saw my willingness to obey His calling, He gave me the strength I needed to go. God gave the invitation, but I needed to accept it. God will never make us do anything we don't want to do, but believe me, if I hadn't gone that afternoon, it's hard to tell where I would be today. I don't even want to think of that.

As the music started, I told my son I wanted to stand. He asked if I was able, and I nodded. He helped me to slowly rise up from the wheelchair, and I raised my hands in praise to God. There was a feeling in the church that day I hadn't felt before, ever. The Spirit of God was there to move for those who had come expecting miracles, and I was one of them.

As the choir sang, I could feel my body beginning to tire to the point of near collapse. I wanted to sit down so badly, but the wonderful feeling inside of me was more than I wanted to forfeit, so I continued to stand. I had to use one hand on the back of the seat in front of me to steady myself, but the other one remained in the air as I praised God for His mercy and grace and thanked Him for bringing me to church that day. I was flooded by the love of God from head to toe. I felt His Spirit more strongly than I ever had before, and I knew it was only a matter of time before He healed me. How can a person be in God's presence like I was that day and not be healed?

Standing there, lost in worship, I heard God speak into my spirit, Mark 5:34, "Daughter, thy faith has made thee whole." I received my healing as soon as He spoke those words to me. I began to feel something else in my chest where the cancer was, and I knew it was God performing my miracle. By this time, the tears were pouring down my face, into my mask, and pooling around my chin, but I didn't care because I was caught up in Him. His presence was so strong on me I wondered why we even fight to live if this was even a ten thousandth of a percent of what Heaven feels like. How glorious a place it must be and how much I badly I want to be with Him. But on the flip side, no one wants to leave their loved ones behind.

I continued to love God, but it had changed from praise to worship. I was worshipping Him for the healing I had just received. No one can convince me God didn't touched me that very day and heal me of the cancer in my body. I knew it was Him, and no one will ever change my mind on that. After worship was over, we took our seats, and I rested during the preaching of the Word. I leaned over and whispered to my son, "God healed me while I was standing up." He looked at me, and I'm sure he didn't know what to think. He was raised in church and attended a private Christian school all of his life, so he knows the power of God and what God can do. I just don't know if he believed me or not. I'm sure he didn't know what to think, but it didn't matter; I believed I was healed, and that's what counted.

When the service was over, I began to tell others God had healed me. They smiled and were happy, but I didn't think they were hearing it in quite the way I was trying to convey it. They seemed pleased, but not ecstatic. Why weren't they as overjoyed as I was? I couldn't figure it out. Maybe they were accustomed to God's healing power, and this was just another one of His miracles. Maybe they didn't believe me. I didn't know, but I wasn't about to stop telling everyone how I had been healed that day.

After the service was over, we came home, and I went straight to bed and slept soundly. I was so exhausted from the day's events that I wanted to crash. When I woke up, I called my friend and told her what had happened and how I was healed. She was more than happy to hear the news, and she praised God along with me.

In life, you will always have those whose faith is as deep as yours, and you will have those who might not have as much faith as you do. But you can't be upset when they don't seem to believe what you say about God and His ability to heal; you just have to live out your relationship with Him in front of them and let them see it for themselves. You can't make people believe something until they are ready to receive it for themselves. I've never been one to shove Jesus or the Bible into someone's face. I will talk about Him all day long, but I won't ever try to make someone believe what I do; that is something that comes from the Holy Spirit alone.

Over the next few months, every time someone asked me how I was doing, I quoted that passage of Scripture to them from Mark. It belonged to me now and was my very own verse that I would cling to from that day forward. I know by now you're probably asking if I ever doubted my healing. The short answer is no. I never doubted for one second that the Lord healed me that day.

Did the enemy try to get me to doubt? Yes, he did. That's what he does. He goes around as a roaring lion, seeking whom he may devour (1 Peter 5:8). But we must be sober and vigilant, continuing always in faith. We must stand firm on the promises of God and believe every word in the Bible. In Isaiah 55:11, God tells His people that His Word which goes from His mouth will not return empty to Him, but rather it will accomplish what He has meant for it to accomplish and will prosper in the thing for which it was sent. That is powerful! When God says something, we can believe it to be true. So when God says He is a healer, you CAN believe it! He wants us to be made whole.

If you are seeking a miracle healing from God today, ask Him, trust Him, and obey Him when He says to go. Stand firm in your faith in Him and what He can do. It could be the difference between getting your miracle and staying in the place you are at this very moment.

Fourteen

God's Purpose for My Life

"Let your light so shine before men, that they may see your good works, and glorify your Father which is in Heaven."
-Matthew 5:16

When I first gave my heart to God—I mean when I totally surrendered my entire heart, soul, mind, spirit, life, and will to Him—I told Him I would do whatever He called me to do. And I meant what I said. I wanted to work for Him. I wanted to tell others about His mercy and how if He could take a rotten person like me and completely transform me, then He could do anything for anyone. I wanted others to see in Him what I do and to know Him like I do. But how? How would I go about telling everyone I could about this man, Jesus?

CANCER, GOD, AND ME

I couldn't sing, so that was out. I couldn't preach, so that wouldn't work either. I wasn't famous, so spreading the gospel to millions of people was out as well. But there was one thing I was good at, and that was writing. In my former life (when I was a sinner) I used to write books that weren't so nice. They were romance novels, and they definitely weren't anything that uplifted God, that's for sure. However, I knew I had a gift in putting my feelings and thoughts onto paper, and I decided to use that for God. I promised Him in 2017 that from then on I would use the talents He had given me for Him and the uplifting of His Kingdom. In July 2019, I released my devotional, Speak Life. It's a thirty-one day devotional that uses God's Word to help an individual build a better and deeper relationship with Him. I had been working on a second one in my spare time before cancer, but once I was diagnosed, everything in my life seemed to be put on hold. I was deeply upset by that, but I soon found out that God had a plan for my life after all (and you all know how I love plans).

As you have read by now, right after my diagnosis, I began my cancer blog on Facebook. I would write poems (that was before chemo brain, which is real by the way) and write about my daily activities, feelings etc. I began to write blog posts that were a little longer than the normal blog should be, but I found they didn't get much traffic on my page like the shorter posts did. I realized people are extremely busy in their daily lives, and they simply don't have time to sit and read a lengthy post on social media. That's when the idea of this book was born, but that's a story for another day (or chapter). At any rate, I felt God wanted me to continue to reach out to people and share what He was doing and who He is. But if they weren't going to read it, why write it, right?

Well, one day, God spoke to me and led me to do a video and say the same thing in it that I would normally say in a blog post.

A video?! I thought. Why would I do a video when I don't like seeing myself on camera or in pictures? Well, I've learned that you don't argue with God. You just do what He asks and obey His voice. So I made some notes, propped up my phone on my coffee table, and made my first video about His goodness. I spoke about how He is there with us when we don't even feel Him and how He will never leave us. I read numerous passages from the Bible and even shared my personal experiences regarding that subject and my cancer. I posted it to my page, and a few people viewed it and liked it. I was happy. I mean, at least a few people, however little the number was, watched it. I know enough about God's Word to know we're supposed to be content with where we are at the moment, and when God decides it's time to move on, then He will bring about the necessary change in our lives. I also know He tells us we're not supposed to despise small beginnings (Zechariah 4:10). Everyone has to start somewhere. I've always believed that when an individual bursts out of the gate at warp speed, then goes far really quickly, he or she will burn out just as fast. But when one starts small and builds brick by brick, they have the opportunity to obtain the wisdom and knowledge needed to be taken to the next level.

My videos were doing okay. I believed God was allowing them to be viewed by the ones who really needed to see them, and that was enough for me. So I continued to make them. I would make one or two a week and upload them to my page. They were always uplifting, positive, and encouraging. One day it hit me—who needed them more than the women in the breast cancer support group? I mean, they (and I) were going through the darkest time of life, and I realized from my own experience that I seemed to always be looking for survivor stories or someone to lift me up and encourage me to go on another day. It stood to reason that those women probably were as well.

One day I sat down and recorded a video tailor-made

for them. I spoke about how we go through suffering, but how it can be for a purpose. I used Scripture and spoke about God in a way I knew someone needed to hear. I was very nervous before I uploaded it, but I did it anyway. If there is one thing you need to know about me, it's that I do things normal people probably wouldn't do. What I mean by that is, if I want to do something, no matter how harebrained or scary it is, then I do it. Do I always feel like I will succeed? No, I don't, but I do it anyway for the sheer experience of it all.

Take for instance when I worked at Dollywood. I watched all of the shows they had at the park. The singers and dancers made it look so easy, and they were having fun. So one winter day in 2018, I called the head of entertainment (without even knowing him) and asked how I could try to get a part in one of the shows. He told me they were going to have auditions in January (during the off season), and I was welcome to audition. I was thrilled. Was it possible I could be a performer at Dollywood? No way! I can't sing, nor can I dance. But that wasn't going to stop me from making a memory and doing something I knew would be a great deal of fun. Plus, I would one day be able to tell the story of how I auditioned for Dollywood! It was a win-win, even if I lost. So I went for it. I wrote my own song and had some guy who was waiting to audition to play his guitar while I tried to sing. Y'all, when I say this was the funniest thing you've ever heard, I'm not stretching it. It was hilarious. But all of those real performers who were waiting for their turn clapped for me and showed me such support that night. I was given a pink card and told to come back the next day. What? I made the cut, and I was moving forward? Yes, I was. The second day was the dance day, and I knew I was dead in the water, finished before I ever started, but I went anyway. Well, needless to say, I failed miserably because those who were dancing had trained all their lives to do what they were doing. They were half my age, half my size, and half my weight. They were dressed in beautiful flowing dance clothes with their petite little dance shoes, looking like they had just stepped out of a Broadway show. And there I was, dressed in blue jeans, a blouse, and running shoes. I'm laughing so hard just recalling this day as I type. They gave us a very quick lesson with so many steps in the routine I felt as if I should just run away with my tail between my legs before we ever finished learning it. You know that feeling you get when you know you can't do something but you're not a quitter, so you keep going? Well, that's the feeling I had that day. I was going to try my best to remember each part of the routine, and when it was my turn, I was going to do it ... except I wasn't. My group of four was called onto the stage, and I'd forgot every single step they'd taught us. I missed every turn and ended up doing twirls and things that I made up on the spot. I was humiliated, but in a good way. I was sweating and having trouble breathing all while my counterparts were smiling and seeming to float around me like tiny petite butterflies. I felt like the fat caterpillar who never should've left her cocoon that day. We all finished, and I wasn't called ... at all. I've been told that when they need a good chuckle in the office, they stick my tape in, and everyone has a good laugh. And that's perfectly okay with me. I live to bring happiness and laughter to the world. That's just one story of how I have no fear or very little fear when it comes to doing new things.

    I uploaded the video to the breast cancer support group and left it alone. To my surprise, by the end of the day, it had gotten so many views and comments from women who were expressing their gratitude for me speaking encouragement to them. They all told me it was exactly what they needed that day, and I told each of them that it was God and not me. I always make it crystal clear, and I want people to understand that I want NO praise for anything I do because in myself, I can do nothing. It is God who gives me the strength to get up every day and do whatever it is He has called me to do.

CANCER, GOD, AND ME

In making videos for my pink sisters in the breast cancer support group this past year, I have felt such a sense of peace and fulfillment. I know I've finally found my calling, and I am fulfilling the purpose God has for me. All my life, I've had a servant's heart, and I want to help everyone who needs it. I haven't always been able to do that, but it's always been in my heart. With my videos, posts, and now this book, I feel God is taking me deeper into my calling, and nothing makes me happier.

I will explain in a later chapter how God has taken me to another level of helping those who are suffering. God is amazing like that. When we finally let go of all *our* dreams, goals, and wishes for our lives and accept His, then and only then will we find a fulfillment we've never experienced before. Not my will, but thine be done (Luke 22:42).

Fifteen

Hard Days

"Blessed are they that mourn, for they shall be comforted."
-Matthew 5:4

I spent my entire summer in bed because of chemo. My first four treatments were the Red Devil, and they'd left me completely incapacitated. My next twelve treatments were Taxol, which isn't as hard on the body, but comes with problems and side effects of its own. The most problematic side effect of Taxol for me was the neuropathy that developed in my hands and feet. I was told it was a possibility but not a surety. Most women get it, very few do not, so there was a very slim chance I would be blessed and not have to worry with it. But it developed for me anyway, and it was horrible.

Neuropathy is nerve damage that causes numbness,

tingling, and burning sensations in hands and feet. This happens because some chemotherapy medicines can (and most of the time do), cause peripheral nerve damage in the body. With the neuropathy comes an onslaught of other problems as well. So the demon that is nerve damage comes in and brings its evil friends with it. It causes weakness, clumsiness, sharp pains, trouble holding objects such as ink pens, spoons, etc. It also causes oversensitivity to touch, which I'm still experiencing months out from treatment, swallowing difficulties, trouble with balance, and sensitivity to heat and cold, another thing with which I'm still having issues. These are all the reasons I call neuropathy a demon. There are things one can do to relieve the symptoms which include anti-seizure meds (one of which I've been on for years), physical therapy, topical numbing medicines, or stopping the chemo altogether, which is what I had to do eventually. Of my scheduled twelve Taxol treatments, I was only able to receive ten because the neuropathy was so bad that most days I couldn't feel my hands and feet, and was stumbling every time I got up to walk. Which made my chances of falling and getting hurt even greater. It was a vicious cycle. Believe me when I say that I didn't complain when I was told I wouldn't have my last two chemo treatments. Neuropathy can last months, years, or a lifetime if there is enough damage done to the patient's nerves. But I'm happy to say mine has gotten so much better over the past few months. There are still days when I have problems with numbness in my hands and feet, but not to the degree where it was last Fall. I will lie in bed at night, trying to go to sleep, when suddenly a sharp pain shoots through my big toe as if someone just sliced it with a knife. I try to lay as still as possible and trust that this too shall pass. I realize God healed me that day in church, but there were still things I had to go through in order to get to where I am. Epsom salt was of great benefit to me. In my many internet searches of legit articles and those home remedies we cling to just to find relief, I had come across an article that said the salt helped neuropathy. I figured it wouldn't hurt to give it a try. My son already used it for aching muscles, so I didn't have anything to lose. He got me a pack of it, and I began nightly soaks in the tub with a cup of the salt in the water. After the second week, I did begin to feel better. I've been using it for months now, and I swear by it. I'm not saying it's a cure and there might be doctors who disagree with me because the science is not there to back it, but in my experience, Epsom salt was a Godsend for me. I recommend anyone experiencing neuropathy, try it and see if it works for you.

Not only does chemo cause neuropathy, it causes so

many other problems. It would be hard for me to tell you everything without making this book a lot longer than it needs to be. But I will add here some of those horrible things I experienced. These are all normal side effects every single patient goes through. If you are experiencing them, rest assured they are common, but if they become worse or extreme, please call you doctor or go to the emergency room. First, there was the extreme fatigue. I know everyone gets tired, but this is a tired like I've never felt before and never want to feel again. I don't know if I even have adequate words to accurately describe it. It's a tired that's not only in your muscles but deep inside of your body as well. It makes you feel lifeless and on the verge of death. I told you there were three times when I thought I was actually passing away because of the chemo side effects. Well, the fatigue causes you to not even be able to lift your head off the pillow at times.

There is also nausea. I only threw up one time during chemo, and it wasn't bad at all, so I feel very blessed. Some people vomit constantly during treatment, so I was happy not to have to deal with that. I was on two medicines that fought nausea, so instead of taking both of them every eight hours, I would take one every four hours then take the other one every eight hours. That way, I constantly had something in my system, and I feel that warded off any sickness in my stomach that might have come had I not done it that way. If you choose to do this, please ask your doctor first.

I dealt with severe constipation as well, due to the steroids they used before each chemo treatment. I was also on iron pills because I was anemic the entire time during treatment (and I still battle that as of writing this book). The iron pills made it about a million times worse, so I had to start taking a laxative every single day to reverse it and try to maintain a normal bowel routine. Add yet another pill to the already large handful I was taking every morning and night. After the steroids leave your system in approximately three days, the laxatives then turn against you and begin to cause diarrhea, which in turn caused dehydration, which caused seizures that sent me to the ER every other week. It seemed to be never ending. And the sad part was that everything I was going through was common. There was nothing the doctor could do to stop any of it. It was something I had to go through until I was done with treatment.

As if all of those things weren't enough to make me want to throw up my hands and scream, add mouth sores. OH, MY GOODNESS! When I tell you those things were from the pits of Hell, believe it! Mouth sores are caused by chemo that kills bad cells and good cells in your body. The mouth is difficult to heal and fight off germs, so it tends to get infected easily, and therefore you get the sores. The medical term for it is oral mucositis, but I like to call it devil mouth because it's so bad. The doctor informed me it would happen, and I was told I could get a prescription mouth wash to help with it. The sores began on the sides of my tongue and eventually worked their way to my lips, inside my cheeks, to my throat, and finally down my esophagus. That led to not being able to swallow ... anything! I couldn't eat, I couldn't drink, I didn't want anything, and that led to becoming dehydrated once again, to seizures, and back to the ER for fluids. It's a vicious cycle no one truly understands until you've gone through it. I'm not sure if this is common for every chemo patient or not, but those sores worked their way into my nose and ears. I would have nose bleeds every day, and my ears were so sore I could barely touch them. Eventually, I got the mouthwash, and it helped tremendously. It has a numbing agent in it, and every two hours I had to swish and swallow, which was heavenly. It took away the pain for a while at least.

There are so many things that can go wrong during treatment, such as my nails turned black and fell off my fingers. My toenails were so sore I could barely put on my shoes. My eyesight got worse, and now I have a cataract on my right eye because of chemo. I have heart palpitations and a fast heart rate. My blood pressure bounces from extremely low to high on a whim. My thigh muscles were always weak and so were my biceps. The slightest scent of fried food made me want to hurl. I would freeze one minute and sweat the next. My whole body gets prickly, needle-like sensations when I get too hot now. I could go on and on, but I think you get the picture by now that chemo is not easy, and its side effects last a lifetime. It might save your life, but it changes your body from one you had to one you don't really recognize anymore. I don't even want to cover the damage it does to the skin by drying you out from the inside. I will just leave it all here because I think I've made it clear—it's very hard.

There is one very important thing I want to talk about, that I know some of you might be wondering. Why did I continue my treatment if the Lord had healed me? Well, that is a difficult one to explain, so bear with me.

The day I was healed, I texted one of the elders in my

church and told them what had happened. I asked if I should just go ahead and stop treatment because it stood to reason that if I was healed already, I wouldn't need any more medical intervention. I mean, I was healed after all. I was advised to *NOT* stop treatment but to continue on because God uses doctors and medicine to heal our bodies as well. I listened as my friend explained it all to me, and I took her advice. Now, if left to my own devices, I would've just stopped right there, but the elder sister told me something that will always stick with me. She said even though God healed me, there is a purpose to my cancer. That was all the confirmation I needed! Remember in the beginning when I asked God to allow my pain and cancer to be used for the purpose of lifting Him up? Well, here was my chance to uplift Him during the darkest time in my life. I had already been talking to the nurses, doctors, and patients every time I went for an infusion, but I needed to continue. I didn't need to stop before God was finished and everyone had heard about Him.

So I went on with treatment, but I made sure every doctor and nurse knew I was healed and better. When I first told my doctor the Lord healed me, I remember the slight smirk that must have been under his mask because I could see that the corners of his eyes wrinkled, and he seemed amused. I don't know if he is a believer or not, but he sure heard about the Lord each time I talked to him. So did the nurse practitioner, nurses, receptionists, and anyone who talked to me on any given day. I was God's witness on earth, and someone was going to hear about Him.

CANCER, GOD, AND ME

Sixteen

The Exchange
(Trading body parts for my life)

"For by me your days will be multiplied, and years will be added unto your life."
-Proverbs 9:11

Move forward to September 12th, my birthday. That was a day I wasn't sure I would get to see when I thought ahead back in February. But there I was, turning fifty-two, and I was overjoyed about it. Age was always a huge deal for me. The older I got, the more I worried about getting old, if that makes sense. Turning thirty was tough for me mentally because I had grown up thinking life was all about looks, makeup, hair, and clothes. I exercised every day and tried to keep my body in great physical shape. I always stayed somewhere between a size four and six, no matter how grueling the exercise regimen was. I, like most women, had no idea how amazing I was inside and that the outside wasn't what mattered. Women are riddled with self-doubt when it comes to physical appearance, and I was no different. Yep, turning thirty was really tough! It took a mental toll on me that was like trying to get over a hurdle. Then, before I knew it, forty showed up and slapped me in the face. I was maintaining my physical appearance, but it was getting harder to do because with age comes a slower metabolism and those pesky things called wrinkles.

My fiftieth birthday was almost devastating, and had it not been for all my friends who took me to dinner and made me wear a tiara and sash, I would've crawled into bed and slept the entire day away and probably would've eaten an entire pack of Oreos.

But something happened when I turned fifty-two. Something I never experienced before on any other birthday. I was grateful for the first time to have another year under my belt. I was happy to have the chance to announce I was turning fifty-two!! It *was* something to celebrate! Having cancer has helped me to think about things in a different way than I did before. It's okay to get old. In fact, it's more than okay—it's something to be celebrated! It's okay to be bald because even the trees lose their leaves in the winter, but they always come back. And it's okay to have scars because those are the marks of a true warrior. I tried to look at it like this: dead soldiers only have one scar, the one that killed them. I had many, and that meant I was a fighter. It meant something had tried to kill me, but instead of letting it, I kept fighting back. And I would continue the fight until I was the victor.

So, I celebrated my fifty-second birthday with a happy and content heart. I had a peace about it that I had never felt before. I will never look at getting a year older as a bad thing ever again. Instead, I will celebrate it and be glad.

September 23rd, 2020 was the day I had dreaded for months. It was the day a piece of me would be taken away forever, and I would never be the same. When I was first told about the plan of action or treatment plan, mastectomy was a word the doctor included. At first, I was sad, but it was so far out in the span of time I really didn't allow it to enter my mind very often. I was dealing with so many other things in those months that a mastectomy wasn't very high on the list. Honestly, it felt like everything was in slow motion, and the surgery would never get here. I really put it out of my mind ... until I had to.

I continued to take classes all during my journey because I wanted to graduate on time. Granted, I slowed down from full-time to part-time during the last few weeks of spring semester, and I was only going to do part time during the first half of the fall semester. I arranged my classes according to when my mastectomy was tentatively scheduled and so far, everything was going according to plan.

My son and I were at the steakhouse having a late birthday celebration for me with my friend Sharon, when my phone rang. It was the surgeon's office, and I was puzzled as to why they would be calling. The nurse informed me my surgery had been moved up from October 14th to September 23rd and proceeded to give me instructions as to when to get my pre-surgery testing done at the hospital. I waited until she finished and explained to her I simply couldn't have it done then because I had planned all of my classes around the tentative date of October 14th. I told her I would be finished with finals and could have surgery after that with no problem. She said it wasn't possible to wait until then, and it was moved up due to having finished chemo early. She went on to tell me the longer I waited to have the mastectomy, the greater the chances of the cancer returning—triple negative is aggressive like that.

What choice did I have?

Suddenly, it all seemed too real. I hung up the phone and told my son and my friend that surgery was now closer than what I had expected. I no longer had any appetite, so I pushed my steak around on my plate, chopped at my baked potato, and felt worried. I had the original timeline, and I wanted to stick to it. I had my plans, and things were fitting in nicely, so it couldn't be disturbed, right? Wrong. Cancer, chemo, surgery ... none of it waits for me or you. None of those things depend on our schedule or work with us to determine when the best time is to come or go. No, we are completely and totally powerless to them. We are their puppets, doing what they want. They call the shots. That's how it felt to me, anyway. I felt helpless and out of control. And I hated it. But there was no getting around it. I was scheduled for surgery on 9/23/20, and there was no changing it.

The night before my mastectomy, I took a shower so I could wash with body sanitizer they give you pre-surgery. You have to shower with it three days in a row and on the morning of the surgery to ensure, as much as possible, all germs are gone from your body. After I dried off, I stood in front of the mirror and looked at my body. I saw the few scars

I already had, but my body was still basically a real body with all its parts. The ones that were missing were gone from the inside (gallbladder, uterus, ovaries, etc.) and those didn't matter because I couldn't see the empty places they'd left behind. Out of sight, out of mind, right? But my chest was going to look different in less than twelve hours. I was going to be forever changed in ways I still didn't know and would only come to understand as time moved on.

Enter the depression phase of the five stages of grief. If you have never been depressed before, let a surgeon tell you he's about to hack up the best feature on your body and see how it makes you feel. Now, if it seems like I'm being a bit flippant here, I'm not. I will tell you my breasts were always one of the very best features about me. I loved them, and I didn't want to lose them. They were the part of me that fed my baby when he was first born. They were the part of me that I felt identified me as a woman and gave me some amount of self-confidence, and now I was going to lose one or both.

Here I go again with another lecture for those of you who have never been there, so buckle up. If you've never had a mastectomy, please read this very carefully. I hope you'll understand it at least to some extent, but you will never truly grasp what I'm saying. Only those who have experienced the loss of a body part, especially the breasts for women, will know exactly what I'm talking about. Losing your breasts is one of the hardest things you will deal with during the cancer journey. I had someone tell me, "They are only breasts; get over it." I couldn't believe my ears when I heard those words. Needless to say, I unleashed a wrath-filled tongue lashing on her, the likes of which I doubt she'd ever heard before and probably will not hear again as long as she lives. (I have since apologized to her for my hatefulness.) Do NOT ever tell a woman, "They're just boobs; get over it," because if you do you are bringing more pain into that woman's heart. All we want is for someone to offer words of support and encouragement while we deal with this invisible killer called cancer. Please don't tell us to get over something that is going to change the way we look and the way we feel for the rest of our lives. Breasts are a part of the body, just like a leg or an arm, and it's not easy to lose them.

It was the morning of surgery and of course, I was a nervous wreck, again! You all know by now I hate surgery.

But by this time, I had come to trust Dr. C., and I knew I was in good hands.

Once I was changed into my gown and was in the bed, all of the staff began coming in, each doing his or her assigned task. One nurse was asking questions while another was taking vitals, then one was putting in an IV, while someone else was asking me what exactly I was having done. It was all very sterile. I was surprised they had allowed my son to be with me in the room before surgery, because Covid was still a huge deal worldwide. But if he left the room, he could not come back in, so he decided to stay until they took me upstairs. My wonderful son sat there until it was all over.

I was greeted by a pleasant girl with a big smile who introduced herself and said she was taking me to nuclear medicine for the test.

"What test?" I asked her.

"Didn't they explain you have to have the test before surgery?" she asked me.

I shook my head. "No one mentioned I would be having any test beforehand," I told her with worry in my voice.

But it made sense because I had to be at the hospital at 8:00 am, and my surgery wasn't scheduled until noon. That would give them plenty of time to do what they had to do.

She went on to describe what kind of test I would be

getting. They were going to inject some type of dye into my breast, and it would travel to the lymph node and light up the ones that needed to be removed. She told me it would hurt because the doctor was going to put the needle into my nipple. That didn't sound so bad to me because I had already had those half dozen aspirations in the two years prior. Having a needle put anywhere in my body no longer mattered to me. I had concluded that this was going to be a way of life, at least for the next few years.

I was getting ready to have my fifth surgery in less than sixteen months. After all the chemo infusions, lab draws, and pre-surgery pokes and prods, the doctor and his needle didn't scare me at all.

A couple of minutes after she explained what would happen, she happily pushed my bed out the door and took me to the nuclear medicine department down two or three, heck, maybe even five hallways. I don't know. I lost count because all I could think was, "This wasn't part of the plan." Well, at least *I* hadn't known about it.

Almost immediately, the doctor came in to do his part. He inserted a needle into my breast several times and deposited the dye. The nurse then covered me with a warm blanket to allow the medicine to quickly distribute to the lymph nodes before I was to have the test. Incidentally, it did not hurt; she was wrong.

Both of them disappeared through an open door, closing it behind them and leaving me alone in the cold room. In that moment, for whatever reason, the sorrow hit me like a punch to the gut, and I completely broke down into tears. I began to pray and ask God to be with me because I was so afraid. All of the toughness and strength I had up to that point was gone in an instant, and I was completely vulnerable to what was coming at me via my emotions. Where were the uplifting speeches I had given to others? Where was the comfort and encouragement I'd sent to those who were hurting? I couldn't find it for myself in that moment, and it pained me.

When the nurse came back into the room and saw me crying, she handed me a tissue and asked if I was okay. She stood by my side for a moment and offered kind words of comfort. I'm not sure I believed her, but I smiled and said thank you. I appreciated what she was attempting in that moment, but it was going to take me feeling something more than she could provide. She instructed me to get onto the table next to me and told me it would slide into the tube when I was ready. As I was moving over, she asked if she could play Christian music. My heart leaped.

"Of course you can. That's my favorite kind of music,"

I told her. In that one instance, I began to feel a tad bit better. Just knowing I was going to hear songs about Jesus made me feel somewhat uplifted.

Nothing happens by coincidence. God has a grand plan, and everything that comes in our path along the way is part of His plan for our lives. She put her phone on the pillow by my head, and as the music began to play, she slowly slid me into the tube. I had never heard the song before, but it had beautiful lyrics. Ones my spirit needed in that moment. She told me it was called, "Into the Sea" by Tasha Layton. As I lay there very still and unmoving, I listened to every word as she sang. It was exactly what I was feeling. Every single word in that song was every single feeling I was having at that moment. That song spoke to me at the exact time I needed it. One of the lines is "It's gonna be okay." Wow, God's timing is so perfect.

As I lay there in that tube, I felt the presence of God there with me. Please do not take what I'm about to say lightly because it's a serious thing to have God visit us with His presence. I literally could feel God there with me. It was as if I felt Him against my arm. It was such a supernatural feeling and brought me a peace I can't describe. I knew then that everything was going to be alright. And just like the song said, I was going to be okay.

CANCER, GOD, AND ME

When the test was over, the nurse hugged me and told me it was going to be alright. She said she would pray for me, and that meant more to me than she realized. If you ever think that telling someone you are praying for them doesn't matter, you are so wrong. Those words are everything to someone who is at a low point in life.

I was taken back to my room, and within the span of a few minutes I was told my surgery had been moved up because the one before me was cancelled. But wait! That wasn't in my plan. My plan was to have surgery at noon, just like they had told me. I hate surprises, and I hate anything that changes my schedule. I don't like things going off the rails like they seemed to be. First, the date was moved up by three weeks, then the new test I knew nothing about, then the new time for surgery. It was all too much to handle. It was all happening to me, and I had no control.

I hugged my son and told him I loved him as I cried. I watched him try to be strong, knowing all too well he was as scared as I was, but he was holding it together for my sake.

I was taken back to the operating room before I was knocked out, which I hated. I didn't want to see the inside of the place where I was about to be cut open. It was too much to look around and see all of those instruments and big lights above me. I started to shake, literally shake. I was so nervous, not to mention freezing cold, and I asked them to give me something right then and there to go ahead and knock me out; otherwise, I didn't know if I could stay in there watching them prep the room. The anesthesiologist agreed and gave me a small shot of something in my IV. It seemed as if as soon as I asked for it, I was gone. I told you I'm not used to having strong meds.

The next thing I remember is being upstairs in the hospital in my room. I woke up and saw my son sitting in the chair by the window with his laptop. I tried to ask questions, but I was still lingering in the twilight zone for quite a while. Unfortunately, he had given me access to my phone, (not sure if I begged him for it or demanded it; at any rate, I had it) and I made my first post-surgery video. I do not remember doing it, but I saw it the next day. I actually uploaded it to my newsfeed and the support group. That was the funniest and most humiliating video ever. I was still high on the anesthesia, and I was trying to talk through my medicated haze. Oh, how I wish my son would refuse to give me my phone.

I don't remember much of that day, but I had a fairly good night; well, as good as you can in a hospital room. By the next morning, the morphine had worn off, and I was in excruciating pain. The nurse offered another dose of it, and

I took it against my better judgment. I don't like to take anything because I am allergic to so many different types of medicines, and anything new scares me terribly. I was in pain, though, and I needed it.

When she put the morphine in my IV, I felt my heart jump as if it had exploded in my chest. An intense pain shot through my head like a hard thud. I had no idea what had happened, and the way she looked at me when my whole body convulsed, I suspect it scared her too. I told her what I had experienced, and she immediately left the room. When she came back in, she said the doctor told her that happens sometimes when patients aren't used to strong medicines. I have since found out that morphine given in an IV must be administered over a period of 4–5 minutes, very slowly, or the patient could go into cardiac arrest. But she had put it in all at once, with one quick push of the syringe. I have no doubt whatsoever that the grace of God kept me that day. That nurse had no idea what she was doing,! and if God hadn't had a plan and a purpose for me to be here, I would've died right then. After that, I refused every pain shot or pain pill they offered me, and I did my best to make it through my mastectomy recovery with only Tylenol. That was hard settling for a weaker pain reliever, but I did it.

Dr. C. came in around eleven that morning and gave me

the best news I have ever been given.

"I got the pathology report back, and you had a PCR," he said with a huge smile.

I had no idea what those initials stood for, so I asked, "What does that mean?"

"It means pathological complete response."

I smiled from ear to ear. "Is that the same thing as NED?" I asked, hoping he would say yes.

In case you don't know, NED means no evidence of disease. The cancer was all gone.

"It is."

I was overjoyed. I was cancer free, although the doctors don't like to say it that way. They normally wait for five years before they call you cancer free, so I totally understood where he was coming from. I knew God had healed me on June 7th, and I just needed the pathology report to confirm to others that He had in fact taken away the cancer. I left that afternoon and finally came home to begin my healing process. It was going to be a long journey, but it would teach me some valuable lessons.

CANCER, GOD, AND ME

Seventeen

Let the Healing Begin

"The LORD will strengthen him upon the bed of languishing: thou wilt make all his bed in his sickness."
-Psalm 41:3

Once I was home from the hospital, I was sure I would begin to feel better. Everyone knows that trying to get rest in a hospital is virtually impossible. I'm thankful for the nurses who came in and checked on me, but between the pain keeping me awake and then having my vital signs taken every few hours, I barely got any sleep at all. I was really looking forward to being in my own bed and resting. I found out quickly, however, that wasn't going to happen.

The nurses had explained to me I would need to sleep in an upright position after the mastectomy.

"What? Upright? I'm a side sleeper, and sometimes I

roll onto my back and snooze," I replied. They shrugged their shoulders and went on about their business.

Well, I could no longer sleep the way I wanted, at least not until six to eight weeks in the future. I had no idea how I was going to possibly have a restful night while being propped up. The simple answer: I wasn't. It has been five months, and I'm still not sleeping well, or at all, most nights.

A couple of my extended family members came down to help me out for a few days. Family is everything, and when we're young, we tend to take them for granted. But the older we get, the more we realize just how precious they are to us. I'm so thankful I have them in my life. If you have people who love you and are willing to take time out of their day to spend it with you, be grateful because not everyone is blessed with family. I lost my mom in 2005, and there's nothing I wouldn't have given to have her there with me during this ordeal, holding my hand, giving me hugs.

I did really well once I got home. The pain was tolerable, and I only had to take Tylenol a couple of times to alleviate what little aching I still had, which really surprised me. Before surgery, I had an image in my head that I would be writhing and crying with excruciating, debilitating pain and believe me, it wasn't like that at all. If you're facing a mastectomy, please be assured it's not as bad as what you think it will be. And if you're unsure, just ask another cancer patient who has already gone through it. They will tell you the fear of it is far worse than the actual procedure and healing process itself.

The day after I was home, I cooked a delicious meal of roast, potatoes, and cornbread. I had help with lifting the stockpot, of course, but I did the majority of it by myself. Physically, I excelled. Mentally and emotionally, well ... that was another story entirely, a very sad story.

Losing your breasts is perhaps the most painful part of the journey for the majority of women. I rarely hear women say they are glad they a mastectomy. Don't get me wrong, I am glad to have had it because it was part of the measures taken to save my life. But it is a double-edged sword. In one way, it's a good thing; in another way, it's truly the worst thing that a woman can experience.

Whether we like it or not, or whether we're willing to admit it or not, breasts are the symbol of womanhood. Think otherwise? Well, let me prove it to you. In every lingerie ad you see, what is the main part of the body they feature? Breasts. There are push-up bras, sports bras, bralettes, wonder bras, support bras, minimizers, and maximizers. Breasts are given to us as a means to feed our offspring, but they have been turned into the most erotic part of the body by men; men in suits who sit in the offices of advertising agencies and come up with ways to get other men, and even women, to buy their products. And they use breasts to do so. Women all over the world get implants to make their breasts bigger because they believe the lie that having big breasts will enhance their beauty or self-esteem. Some women put a bit of dark eyeshadow between them to give the illusion they are bigger. Heck, even as little girls, we realize the effectiveness or importance of our breasts because if we're flatter than our friends at school, we tend to want to stuff our bras. So, yes, breasts are the symbol of womanhood, for better or worse! Like it or not!

If they are the symbol of who we are as women, then you can imagine how hard it is for us to lose one or both of them. I can only truly speak for myself when I say this was the hardest part of my journey. As I said earlier, I had always kept my body in great physical condition, until the last couple of years when I started to come to terms with who I am as a child of God and not just as a woman. Once I truly found my identity in Christ, it was easier to not allow myself to be consumed with my appearance. I still wanted to dress nicely and look good, but it wasn't something I was constantly thinking about; I had other things that were more important than fancy clothes, perfect makeup, and the much-desired hourglass figure. My thoughts and focus were on such things as praying for others, reading the Bible, and my relationship with God. But even in all of that, losing a part of my body I had always placed a huge emphasis on, and one that made me feel attractive, was almost too much for me to bear.

I am a single woman and have been for more than twelve years. I don't actively date or seek to date because I already have a very full life with college, church, writing, my foundation (which I will explain in the next chapter), and now dealing with breast cancer. Having the mastectomy has brought a lot of mental anguish as far as what it will mean to someone if I ever do decide to date and want to get married. How do you tell a man what your body looks like without clothes on? *When* do you tell him? Do you do it up front so there's no surprises, or wait until there is a solid relationship and he can handle it? But in doing that, is it fair to have him on the hook already and then spring it on him that your chest looks more like a rag doll that has been sewn together with all of its scars instead of what he's used to seeing in Victoria's Secret ads or on beaches?

Those are all valid concerns of a cancer survivor who has had a mastectomy. It all boils down to, "Will I ever be attractive again?"

I want to add this caveat: I chose to not have reconstruction. I felt that my body, mind, and emotions had already gone through enough trauma without adding more surgeries. To have implants after a mastectomy requires a woman to have expanders put in between the skin and chest muscle. They are gradually filled with saline solution over a period of weeks or months until they have stretched the skin enough so that permanent implants can be put in where the expanders were (verywellhealth.com)[5]. That's two surgeries right there that I do not want to have to undergo.

Another option was the Latissimus dorsi flap procedure, and it was the surgery suggested for me if I chose reconstruction. This is where tissue from the upper back is taken to make breasts. OUCH! No, thank you! I mean, come on, they are going to cut up my back and leave scars so I could have breasts? Ummm, I'll pass.

Another option is the deep inferior epigastric perforator or DIEP flap procedure. This is where the doctor takes tissue from the patient's abdomen and uses it to build breasts. If I were going to have any one of them, I would more than likely choose that one. The way I figure, it's the most efficient. They take the tissue from your stomach and then pull it tightly and close it up, thus creating a tummy tuck, all while enhancing your breast. Two birds, one stone. Voilà! You have a new flat stomach and new boobs! Those are both pros, but the con is, it's surgery and as you know by now, I hate surgery. I feel like I keep repeating that over and over, but I want to drive home the point of just how frightened I am of being put to sleep.

You can find more information on these surgeries by visiting the website cancer.org.

My family stayed with me for a few days. Before they left, they helped change my bandage. My sister-in-law and her aunt got all of the gauze and pads ready, put on their gloves, and proceeded to unwrap me after I took off my shirt.

I looked like a mummy, wrapped tightly around my entire chest with a pink binder that closed with Velcro. A binder is a small piece of material that looks more like a tube top from the 70s, and it fits tighter than skin and helps to keep the swelling to a minimum after surgery and before the drain tubes come out. I feel like the binder did me more harm than good. It kept pushing on the tubes coming out of my side and causing them to hurt.

I had already told them I didn't want to look down after

the dressing was off my wound because there was no way I could handle looking at my new body that soon. I think I would've broken down at that point, and I wasn't ready. I know myself well enough to know what causes me to get depressed, and if it's bad enough, I'm afraid I would have a hard time coming out of it like I did when my mom died. I was depressed for almost two years after she passed away. It was a terrible time in my life, and I try not to go there if I can help it.

They carefully peeled off the bandage, and I could feel the air hitting my chest. I knew it was exposed, and so I kept my gaze on the ceiling fan in my bedroom as I let them do for me what I should've been doing for myself ... except I couldn't. Where was the strong woman I used to be? She wasn't able to deal with what was happening at that moment in life.

Once I was completely undone, I heard my sister-in-law say it looked good for what it was, and the scar wasn't going to be that bad. To say I was relieved was an understatement. Her words in that second were what kept me from falling apart. They were exactly what I needed to hear. The Bible tells us about how words fitly spoken are like apples of gold (Proverbs 25:11). They are precious and good for us.

CHRISTY ADAMS

They had managed to cheer me up during a very rough time that day, and I appreciated it more than they knew. After they left, however, was going to be another story. I would have to do it for myself, and that was something I wasn't sure I could do.

A couple of days later, when it came time to change the dressing again, I needed my son to help with the binder. He happily obliged, and he and I worked together to unwrap me. I told him I didn't want to see myself because I wasn't ready to face what I looked like. He told me if I would hand him the supplies, he would gladly change the bandages. I was relieved. We began, but all didn't go as we had planned. He somehow managed to drop the bandages, and I instinctively looked down to catch them. To my dismay, I saw the huge scar that was now the replacement of my womanhood, and I was devasted. I quickly looked up at the ceiling and began to cry. It was more than I could handle. I wanted to run away, but I couldn't. I was changed, scarred, and mutilated. I was disgusting and gross. How could anyone ever find me attractive again? How would I ever be able to look in the mirror again? Those were the questions bombarding my mind and emotions. I wanted to go to sleep and forget what was happening.

CANCER, GOD, AND ME

Poor body image after getting a mastectomy is something all women deal with on a daily basis. But one study suggests that women who have breast conserving surgery have a more positive body image than those who didn't have any type of reconstruction. (Stavrou, et al, 2009)[2] That makes sense because, as I just explained, our breasts are a huge part of who we are as females.

Not only do we face such an abrupt change in how we feel physically, but shopping habits must also change. I went from having to buy extra-large shirts because of my 36DD breasts to now being able to wear a medium. None of the shirts I had in my closet fit the way they used to, and it seemed as if everything I put on now looked terrible. As soon as I would try a piece of clothing on, I became angry and took it off and threw it on the bed. The frustration of trying to find something to wear was so overwhelming I would simply cancel my plans altogether. Staying home in my pajamas was easier.

One of the hardest things I did after surgery was putting away all of my pretty bras. I no longer needed them. I've never been one to spend a fortune on clothes, in fact, as soon as I go into a store, the first place I head to is the sales rack. But my undergarments were another story. I didn't care to pay $75 for a bra if it fit me right. There was one certain type from Victoria's Secret I had to buy because it was not only comfortable, but it provided full coverage as well. Knowing I was never going to wear them again was heartbreaking. The bra I wear now is more like something you'd expect to find in the old ladies department from the 1950s. It comes equipped with very heavy silicone prostheses that helps me look normal in my clothes. I am thankful for the prosthetic, but I wish I could just have my old body back.

It's been five months since surgery, and I have healed a bit more. The initial trauma is over but I'm still learning how to cope with all the physical and lifestyle changes I've had to go through. I have thought about reconstruction, but the fear of yet another surgery and all the risks outweigh any benefits I can find. Who knows, one day I might change my mind and decide to take the plunge, but until then, I'll have to remain who I am, just the way I am.

CANCER, GOD, AND ME

Eighteen

Close to My Heart

"But whoso hath this world's good, and seeth his brother have need, and shutteth up his bowels of compassion from him, how dwelleth the love of God in him?"

-1 John 3:17

There are times in life when we all feel we want to be on an island, live to ourselves in isolation and not be bothered with people and their problems. But inside our hearts is a button, and when pressed it causes us to leap to the aid of our fellow man. It's because we all have a purpose in our lives. We were created to do something; more importantly, something that helps others.

Perhaps the most well-known case of this was when Jesus fed the multitude with a boy's lunch. In Matthew 14, we are told of how He took a boy's five loaves of bread and two fishes and multiplied them so that more than 5,000 people could eat. The Bible makes it clear there were over 5,000 men, in addition to the women and children. He could have said, "Well, you guys knew you'd need something to eat; why didn't you pack a lunch before you came?" Instead, He had a deep compassion for them and worked a miracle. He took what the little boy had and made enough for everyone to eat.

We see examples of this time and again when natural disasters hit our country. When a flood, tornado, hurricane, or out of control forest fires come unexpectedly, Americans jump in and help each other by volunteering, sending supplies, or donating money. We all work together to ensure our neighbors have what they need to survive. That, my friend, is compassion. Merriam-Webster states compassion is "The sympathetic consciousness of other's distress together with a desire to alleviate it." When people are in trouble, there is something that rises up in us to want to be of aid to that person or group of people, so they feel comfort.

This brings me to what this chapter is all about. During my journey, I couldn't have made it without my friends and family who pitched in and helped me. As I stated in the beginning of the book, on the day I received my diagnosis, I

CHRISTY ADAMS

was told not to come back to work. My boss laid me off, and I wasn't able to get unemployment because to receive that in the state of Tennessee, you have to be able-bodied enough to look for and accept work. I was getting ready to begin my surgeries and treatments, so I wasn't going to be able to work.

But through the help of the health department and my doctor, I was able to get all my healthcare covered by the Breast and Cervical Cancer Prevention and Treatment Act (BCCTPA) that was passed in 2000, so that was a massive load off my mind. Paying my bills, however, was still an issue. I trusted God to take care of us, though. He always had and always will. Immediately after my diagnosis, without me even asking, people started pouring into my life. They offered prayer, love, support, financial blessings, and gifts of all sorts. I had a friend buy me a brand-new recliner so I could sleep comfortably during the treatment process; that was a Godsend. I had a friend who paid my rent for one month, almost $700 dollars, and never expected to be paid back. I mean, who does that? I will tell you who—good people with good hearts that love me, that's who. I had a friend who made up a care package basket and brought it to me that contained hand sanitizers, slippers, a book, and other sweet items that brought me comfort. She included a card with money as well. I had people sending me bracelets and socks, among other things that touched my heart on a daily basis. I wore every piece of jewelry, every cap, every clothing item, and the money was used to pay our bills. I am so thankful for those who jumped in when I needed it the most and helped me out during one of life's hardest crises.

Right in the middle of my journey, while I was still taking chemo, I felt the Lord leading me to start a non-profit organization to help breast cancer patients get the essential items they would need during their own treatment. Sometimes, we don't know a need exists until we have it ourselves. By that time, I knew how great the necessity was, but I was going to have to figure out how to help.

As with all ideas I have, I put it on the back burner so when I revisited it later on, I would know whether or not it was only a thought I had in passing, or something God was truly leading me to do. So I put it aside and never thought about it much. Occasionally, it would enter my mind, and I would say, "Lord, let me think about it a little longer."

After my chemo ended in late August, the desire to start the foundation was still there, and I knew it was indeed God who was bidding me to put it together. So I emailed a friend who had started his own non-profit organization several years earlier and asked him to explain the ins and outs of it all. I had zero knowledge of where to even begin. He happily emailed me back with the starting point, congratulated me, and with that I was off. I began to research every facet I could regarding non-profit organizations and charities. It was all new to me, and so much of the language was about things I didn't understand at the time but would come to learn in the following months. I did everything I was supposed to do as far as state and federal paperwork were concerned, got my articles of incorporation, my employer identification number, and filed for a tax-exempt status. My son built the website, I ordered supplies, and with that, *Close to My Heart Breast Cancer Foundation* was born in late September 2020! I was ecstatic. I was on my way to helping breast cancer patients get the things they needed during treatment.

I made a Facebook page for the organization and invited friends to like and follow it. After a couple of days, donations started pouring in faster than I had ever dreamed they would. In the beginning, I was hoping to help at least five women each month with care packages filled with items they needed. The staples would include a mask, throw, journal and pen, a tote bag, chemo cap, and lip balm. There are also other items the patient can get if they are facing a mastectomy, such as a mastectomy pillow and shirt, along with a lanyard to hold their drain tubes after surgery.

Not only did I receive monetary donations, but people

began to send things they made, such as beanies and caps. I also got donations from women who were selling makeup and nail kits. My heart was overjoyed. To think that other people would share in my vision of helping those who were suffering brought tears to my eyes.

I am happy to report that in just five short months, we were able to far exceed my goal of helping five patients a month to helping a total of fifty-nine patients since we started in mid-October 2020.

As I said earlier, I've always had a servant's heart, and I've always known that part of my calling and purpose on earth was to help others. This foundation came along at the exact right time in my life. I know, that for myself, when I am sick, I want to pray for others who are ill. When I am lonely, I pray for those who are lonely too. So when I was struggling with everything during my journey, I wanted to help those women who were struggling too. I've found when I take the focus off myself and put it onto others, my problems don't seem as bad. The Bible speaks of this somewhat in Romans 12:10 when it states, "Be kindly affectionate to one another with brotherly love, in honor giving preference to one another." In other words, Paul was saying to love each other as you would love your sibling and give honor to each other before you would honor yourself.

Well, in my times of sickness, I want to pray for others and honor them. And in my times of struggle, I wanted to honor others by helping them with the items they need but might not be able to afford.

The things in the care packages aren't meant to be lifesaving items, but they are useful items that I hope will bring a smile to the face of a woman who is suffering the worst battle in her life. If I can do that with one box full of pink things, then I believe I've fulfilled my calling on this earth. Like the verse says, whoever sees someone in need but shuts up his or her bowels of compassion can't very well say they have the love of God in them. I strive every day to be the extension of God's love here on Earth. I pray I am successful each time I try.

I will include ways to donate to the foundation at the end of the book. If you feel led to give to this foundation, please do so; it will mean a lot to every patient who receives a care package.

CANCER, GOD, AND ME

Nineteen

I'm Zapped!

"I have fought a good fight, I have finished my course, I have kept the faith."
-2 Timothy 4:7

There was to be one more step before I reached the end of treatment: radiation. I dreaded it too. I hated even the very sound of the word. Say it out loud right now. Radiation. YUCK! It brings to mind images of red peeling skin that is painful to touch. Heck, it even conjures up thoughts of danger in my mind. I mean, how many of us have ever seen the red wording in an x-ray room with warnings of how harmful radiation is? How dangerous it must be if the technician has to leave the room, for Pete's sake! It wasn't something I was overjoyed about having put into my body.

I remember when my grandfather had throat cancer and

had radiation. He drove two hours one way every day to get zapped. After forty-five treatments, he couldn't swallow any food unless it was pureed or already soft, such as mashed potatoes or soup. He passed away in 2005 of lung cancer that had metastasized to his brain. He was already too far gone, but the doctor did radiation treatments anyway to give him a little more time. I remember his poor bald head being burned so badly that my heart broke for him. He eventually stopped having treatments and decided he wanted to live out whatever days he had left with no medical intervention at all. I can't say I blame him. I mean, it wasn't going to do him any good, and it wasn't worth the time he was spending traveling. He wanted to be in his home, surrounded by his family in his last days rather than delay the inevitable.

I went into it with some knowledge already of what to expect from the radiation treatments. I was scheduled for thirty-one treatments, and I dreaded every single one of them. I even talked to my oncologist about how important it was to get them. I was healed, after all! There was no evidence of disease, so why get the radiation?

He told me, "Just in case there are microscopic cancer cells that are undetectable."

I shrugged my shoulders and reluctantly agreed to have it. "Okay, fine."

CHRISTY ADAMS

I figured there must be someone there who needed to hear my testimony. Up to that point, I told everyone I had come in contact with about the Lord and how good He is, and I wasn't about to stop. I had made a promise to God that I would use this horrendous battle for His glory, to uplift Him and what He can do, and I wasn't about to stop.

My treatments started in early November and were scheduled daily, with the exception of weekends and holidays. I should've finished just before Christmas, except I kept missing each week. Some of those missed treatments were because I was too sick to leave the house, and one was because there was a roadblock in traffic one day, so I turned around and drove home. The truth is, I didn't want to go. I despised getting them. It was almost as if I was reliving the denial phase of the stages of grief, just like I had done before going to see the surgeon. The actual treatment itself didn't hurt. I didn't even feel it when it was happening. The worst part about it was that I had to go every day, and I was already exhausted from chemo, surgery, and the mental toll cancer had all taken. I just wanted to stop, but I couldn't. I had to see it through to the end. Each and every day I went, I tried to share the goodness of God with those I talked to, and I think it did some good. One lady had lung cancer, and she wasn't doing very well. I hope I was able to give her some amount of hope by sharing the gospel with her. Only God knows because I never got her name. We spent each day in a very small waiting room separated by a tiny end table, and I never asked her name. I just told her about God.

Toward the end of my treatments, I began to burn. I was surprised it hadn't happened before then. It started out as a redness and quickly turned black. My entire chest, neck, side, armpit, and stomach had turned pitch black, and it hurt terribly. Each time I looked at it, I was reminded of a steak that I had left on my grill a little too long one sunny afternoon a few years ago. I know that sounds gross, but my skin was literally charred!! The pain was so terrible that even my softest t-shirt caused me to shriek when it laid against my flesh. That was all the more reason that I wanted to quit. I wanted to stop going and allowing my body to be treated like some science experiment! It was enough!!! I was sick of it all!! I just wanted it to be over, but I couldn't stop. I had to keep going back. I had to keep returning to the place where I was being burned for "my own good."

Isn't it weird how the thing that hurts us the most is the thing that also saves us? The medicine that kills the intruder in our bodies also damages us to the point of being unrecognizable, but it's for our own good. It's necessary. During the process, it's the hardest thing that we have ever endured but in the end, it's all worth it. If we can just endure to the end, then there is celebration and joy. But during the trial, it's hard to hold on.

I finally finished my treatments in mid-January, and I couldn't have been happier. During the last leg of my journey, I felt as if time was limping along at a snail's pace. No, slower than a snail's pace. It felt as if the clock had slowed down, and the days were twice as long than before. All I wanted was to be done and begin to heal and move on. All I wanted was to forget about it all and get my life back on track.

On January 15th, I received my certificate for completing radiation, had my picture taken with the sweet nurses, said my goodbyes, and got out of there. I was home free! I was finished. I had done it; my treatments were over.

Now what?

CANCER, GOD, AND ME

Twenty

It's Over… Now What?

"But thanks be to God, which giveth us victory through our Lord Jesus Christ."

-1 Corinthians 15:57

    I reached the end of my journey. The final bell rang, and I had triumphantly stepped to the center of the ring and raised my arms in victory. I was the winner! I had beaten the enemy that was sent to take me down. I looked over and saw my opponent lying on the floor in defeat. I was crowned the champion, and it felt amazing!

    It's really something to look back at the path I've walked in 2020-2021 and remember in detail all those things that happened to me. Writing this book was very therapeutic, and it caused me to smile and to cry at times. But I'm so happy to have the ability to delve into it and sort it all out. I

CANCER, GOD, AND ME

pray it will help other breast cancer patients and survivors to know what they're going through is only one more battle in your life. It doesn't define you unless you allow it to do so. With hope, faith, and family, you and Jesus can win it. You can come out on the other side a victor.

When I began my journey, I knew one thing—I didn't want to be another statistic. I didn't want to be just a memory of a pink fighter. I wanted to be a survivor, so I had to fight with everything I in me. We've all heard the saying "Fight like a girl." Well, some people are offended by that, but not me. As a woman, I love that saying because it shows just how tough women are. If someone is telling you to fight like a girl, take it as a compliment. Women bring life into this world. Women overcome stereotypes of being the weaker sex. Women climb the corporate ladder while taking care of homes, children, and husbands, proving they're just as strong as what society deems men to be. All the while, we really *are* stronger. So when someone says, "Fight like a girl," I will. And I'll win every time because girls are tough!

The fight isn't completely over, only that particular battle. There will be doctor visits every three months, mammograms every six months, and MRIs every so often, for the next five years. Oh, and that pesky little thing called fear will try to sneak into my mind occasionally and cause me to think about recurrence.

Triple negative has the highest recurrence rate of all types of breast cancer, and it has the lowest prognosis too. But hey, the Lord showed it who was boss in 2020, and He can do it again *if* it ever decides to rear its ugly head once more. When those thoughts come, and they do because I'm human, I push them out of my mind and live each day to the absolute fullest. I spend time with my son playing our favorite game, UNO, and laughing at silly jokes that only he and I understand. I spend time with my little dog, Abby, telling her how much I love her for being so loyal to me during my ordeal. I make it a point to talk to my sister and my friends *every single day*. With all those things to do, I don't have time for fear to try to find a place in my mind and life.

The Bible tells us we all have an appointed time to die, and after that, the judgment (Hebrews 9:27). If cancer has taught me one important lesson this past year, it's that I nor anyone else will leave this earth until our time is over. When God says it's time to go, no one can stop it. So I will live without fear of the future but rather fill each day with happiness and joy.

'*She is clothed with strength and honor; and she shall rejoice in time to come. She opens her mouth with wisdom*

CANCER, GOD, AND ME

and in her tongue is the law of kindness."
  -Proverbs 31:25-28

Epilogue

I want to finish this book by trying to explain how cancer has changed me. I hope you will hear my heart as you read my words.

When you have an evil disease like cancer inside of you that is growing every day and its cells are dividing faster than you care to think about, you realize just how quickly and easily something can take you out of this world. So, you go into fight or flight mode. For those who choose to fight, something happens in your mind lets you know it's time to toughen up and put on your armor. You're going into combat, after all. So, you take up your sword and your shield, walk onto the battlefield, and begin the daunting task of fighting the war to live.

It's not pretty, it's not nice, and it's definitely not a walk in the park. It's ugly, cruel, and grueling. Every day you make conscious and unconscious decisions that will affect the war that has been waged against you. Everything changes. You look at everything in life differently than you did before. Small things do not matter, and pettiness is no longer an issue. No, you've got bigger things that need your attention…such as living. You don't bother with childish arguments and frustrations. Now you are in the ring with an enemy so strong that if you so much as turn your head slightly and look away, it will knock you out for good. So, you pay attention to its every move and you're always on guard for the next punch or hit.

Then one day, you wake up and the battle is over; the enemy is gone, and you are the winner. You are beyond happy about it. But things seem to be different now. You don't *feel* like yourself anymore; you don't *look* like yourself anymore; and you don't *act* like yourself anymore.

People begin to question you as to what happened to the girl they knew just a few months before cancer changed you.

"Why are you different now?" they ask.

"Why do you seem bitter or rude at times?"

I stare at them, knowing what they say is true and knowing deep down that it is something I have to work on. But I shrug my shoulders and answer the only way I can by saying, "I *am* different now".

CHRISTY ADAMS

Cancer changed me, as it does everyone who has battled it or will ever battle it. It literally changed me in a way that not many people realize. If I have a hardness about me now or if I seem short or unrelenting, it's because the ugly disease caused me to put up my fists and fight *every* day. And if I still seem as if I'm on guard and come off as rude at times, it's nothing personal toward anyone, I promise. It's just the residual effects of having had to fight so hard for an entire year just to get out of bed some days or just to try and feel human again.

The thought of keeping myself in a place of strength mentally and emotionally in case it ever comes back is very tiring as well. I want to be ready just in case that monster decides to rear its ugly head again. But how do I ensure that my anger for the cancer doesn't spill over into my daily life and onto those who love me? Well, that's where I walk a thin line. I have to use prayer, Scripture, and my relationship with God every day and then it's still a battle some days.

PTSD (post-traumatic stress disorder) is very real among women who have been diagnosed with breast cancer. I'll link a study that showed more than 82.5% of women who have had breast cancer still experience PTSD symptoms more than one year after diagnosis. Those symptoms include, but are not limited to, flashbacks, feelings of detachment, being emotionally numb, sudden outbursts of anger, and being upset at minor things that might not upset most people (breastcancer.org).

I pray every day that none of those symptoms find their way into my friendships, family relationships, or casual acquaintances but I cannot promise they won't. But please know that me and God are still working on that… every, single, day.

Once cancer and anger have invaded you, both are hard to get rid of. The cancer is gone but you must let the anger go as well. The anger was always meant for the cancer, but sometimes it found its way to those I love the most.

I'll never be the same Christy you once knew but I hope the woman I am now can be an even better version of who I was before cancer fought me and lost.

Blessings to you all,
Christy Adams
Daughter of God
Breast Cancer Warrior and Survivor

CHRISTY ADAMS

Close to My Heart Breast Cancer Foundation

Close to My Heart

Breast Cancer Foundation

About Us

We are a non-profit organization founded in October 2020, by breast cancer survivor Christy Adams.

We are made up of a team of caring individuals who are committed to helping those who suffer from breast cancer as well.

Our board members include people from all walks of life who know the importance of reaching out to those who need a helping hand. We feel blessed to be a part of this organization.

What We Do

We provide comfort and peace of mind by way of supplies and necessary items for women who need a little extra help during their own journey through cancer. We might not be able to meet every need, but it is our belief that by helping in any way we can, the burden might not be as heavy.

We are all in this life together.

Contact Us:
Close to My Heart Breast Cancer Foundation
c/o Christy Adams
325 Chestnut Ridge Way
Newport, TN 37821

closetomyheartfoundation@gmail.com
www.closetomyheartfoundation.weebly.com
www.facebook.com/closetomyheartbreastcancerfoundation

CHRISTY ADAMS

Donations can be made via:

PayPal at:

paypal.me/closetomyheartbcf

closetomyheartfoundation@gmail.com

Venmo at:

Venmo.com/closetomyheartfoundation

Cash App:

$closetomyheart

Or by mailing a check or money order to the address above.

About the Author

Christy Adams is first and foremost a Christian who loves the Lord more than anything else in life. She is the author of five books. Her last book, Speak Life, released in July 2019 and reached #1 on Amazon in its category of Prayer/Devotionals just after its release and then climbed to #1 again in 2020.

She has also appeared on The Dr. Phil Show, Daytime Blue Ridge, and WVLT, sharing her experiences and the goodness of God.

Christy has a son, Joshua, who resides with her in the beautiful Smoky Mountains of East Tennessee. She also is the proud mom of her fur baby, Abby.

She is a graduate of Liberty University where she earned her Bachelor of Science (BS) in Psychology and Christian counseling. She is currently enrolled in the Master of Applied Psychology program at Liberty University in Lynchburg, Virginia.

For fun, Christy likes to ride out to Douglas Lake and relax by the water. Writing books and reading is her passion, so she devotes as much time to that as possible. And she also loves spending time with family and friends and attending church.

References

[1] Nakashima, K., Uematsu, T., Takahashi, K. et al. Does Breast Cancer Growth Rate Really Depend on Tumor Subtype? Measurement of Tumor Doubling Time Using Serial Ultrasonography Between Diagnosis and Surgery. *Breast Cancer*. 2018 Sept 26. (Epub ahead of print). DOI: 10.1007/s12282-018-0914-0

[2] Stavrou, D., Weissman, O., Polyniki, A., Papageorgiou, N., Haik, J., Farber, N., & Winkler, E. (2009). Quality of life after breast cancer surgery with or without reconstruction. *Eplasty*, *9*, e18.

[3] https://www.breastcancer.org/symptoms/understand_bc/statistics

[4] https://www.cancer.org/cancer/breast-cancer/reconstruction-surgery/breast-reconstruction-options/breast--using-your-own-tissues-flap-procedures.html

[5] https://www.verywellhealth.com/

Made in the USA
Monee, IL
05 July 2025